CURSED IN VIRGINIA

STORIES OF THE DAMNED
IN THE OLD DOMINION STATE

Mark Nesbitt

Globe
Pequot

GUILFORD, CONNECTICUT

Globe Pequot

An imprint of Rowman & Littlefield

Distributed by NATIONAL BOOK NETWORK

British Library Cataloguing in Publication Information available

Library of Congress Cataloging-in-Publication Data available

ISBN 978-1-4930-1955-7 (paperback)
ISBN 978-1-4930-1956-4 (e-book)

♾™ The paper used in this publication meets the minimum requirements of American National Standard for Information Sciences—Permanence of Paper for Printed Library Materials, ANSI/NISO Z39.48-1992.

Printed in the United States of America

CONTENTS

INTRODUCTION

A curse, according to Rosemary Ellen Guiley in *Harper's Encyclopedia of Mystical and Paranormal Experience*, is a psychic attack upon "humans or animals that causes physical or mental distress, injury, illness, or even death." Curses can be cast by humans or by nonphysical beings such as spirits, demons, or "thought-forms . . . out-of-body projection of a double or astral form." A curse can be sent by a sorcerer to magically assassinate someone with a medicine-resistant disease or by a "familiar" in the shape of a snake, scorpion, or another deadly animal. Dolls (as in voodoo), or a lock of hair from the target, may also be used to transmit the curse.

By their very nature, curses have a mysterious, supernatural aspect to them. Perhaps that's why we attribute things we don't understand to a curse: happenstance, circumstances, continuing bad weather, bad luck, a dropped ball in a crucial game, a missed shot. "I must be cursed," we say, when the ball slices into the woods for the third hole in a row.

But what about a "classic" curse? How do you know if you've been the victim? One way is by experiencing the "Hag Syndrome," when you awaken in the middle of the night utterly paralyzed with what feels like a heavy weight crushing you. You may also encounter unexplainable bouts with irrational fear, or feelings of dread followed by a nervous breakdown and wasting away unto death. You may suffer from bruises in the morning from nighttime psychic attacks, poltergeist ("noisy ghost") activity such as slamming of doors, moving of objects, or lights flashing on and off, and mysterious signs of an invisible entity, such as footprints, or sudden flash fires erupting with no ignition source.

Casting a curse, it seems, has been around for nearly all of humanity. For a thousand years, between 500 BC until 500 CE, the name of the cursed, of deities or demons requested to carry out the curse, magic symbols, and, of course, the curse itself were written down on curse tablets, or *tabellae defixionum*, and buried in graveyards near the newly interred, on battlefields, or the spot where executions took place. Water, being a psychic element, was also used as a repository for the curse tablets. Archaeologists have found them in abandoned wells, springs, and rivers.

There are several ways of combating a curse, all of which seem impossible to do without making the cure worse than the illness. For one thing, you need to avoid contact with the people or places associated with the curse; do not go near water which, most paranormalists agree, feeds psychic powers; do not let yourself get hungry—hunger allegedly opens the portals to supernatural powers; soak in the sun and its healing energy; do not spend too much time alone; and finally, find someone adept in the occult to perform the appropriate rituals for protection and nullification of the curse.

Curses can go on for generations, afflicting even the innocent. According to some sources, curses can be made simply by wishing ill upon others or having negative thoughts about someone. So be careful what you wish.

You may be cursed by being in a certain family. Not all famous, wealthy families have good luck; some have horrifying events associated with them. Fame doesn't necessarily mean you will escape life curse-free. Notice some wealthy and famous actors or political families who just can't seem to get it together and be happy, or are plagued by early, untimely deaths.

More modern interpretations expand the nature of the curse, and the definition has been stretched a bit.

Objects can be cursed, especially objects used in rituals or in heinous crimes. Weapons used for mayhem can hold a curse and condemn those who find, purchase, or inherit them. Places can be cursed. Even earth objects such as caves or open fields can be considered cursed. Battlefields are notorious for having sites, especially where soldiers were trapped or slaughtered, that repeatedly give people bad feelings or produce strange sightings, photos, and video or audio recordings. Stones, once removed from certain areas—like lava rocks from Hawaii—are said to bring bad luck, although while left in place are innocuous.

Saying "Oh, I'm cursed" doesn't always mean that someone else did it. It can merely mean that a person feels afflicted by a series of bad events that he or she did nothing to bring about, or feel that they don't deserve. In other words, another intangible, supernatural phenomenon—"luck," or lack thereof—has much to do with feeling cursed.

Being cursed can also be one's own fault. To venture into a place of natural danger will greatly increase the chances of having bad luck. Witness America's first settlers in Jamestown, or the British experience in attempting to hold on to their colonies in America, or any of the soldiers of the Civil War who fought on battlefields in Virginia.

Though Virginia, with its placid tidewater rivers, lovely rolling piedmont, lush, fertile Shenandoah Valley, and magnificent mountains should seem more blessed than cursed, it must be remembered that it is the same state which had, acre for acre, more battles than any other place in the United States. Virginia's natural beauty and friendly Southern charm veil a disturbing past.

1

JAMESTOWN: BLESSED OR CURSED?

Americans look back at the 1607 establishment of the first English settlement at Jamestown, Virginia, with great pride, dressing the event as a marvelous adventure undertaken by sublimely courageous individuals destined to carve out a great nation from lush wilderness by hard work and subtle diplomacy with the indigenous Native peoples. With the grace of God they planted a foothold in the New World and made peace with the "Indians," thanks to the beautiful young daughter of a chieftain, who, infatuated with one of the leaders, helped them plant crops and shared hunted game with them so they might prosper.

English minister Reverend William Symonds once said in a sermon that, just as God had called Abraham in the Bible, so had He called the English to America, a sort of latter-day Promised Land.

Or at least this is one version we've been taught.

The real story, however, is quite different, and in some cases, quite shocking.

"The soil was good and fruitful, with excellent good timber. There are also great store of vines . . . in great abundance . . . many squirrels, conies, blackbirds with crimson wings and divers [numerous] other fowls and birds."

That description comes from George Percy, one of the first settlers of what was to become Jamestown, writing about what he witnessed in one of his first sightings of the New World in the spring of 1607. After leaving London on December 20, 1606, and a dreary four-month voyage across the Atlantic, the Chesapeake Bay and its dry-land environs would have looked pretty good in April of 1607—except, of course, for the brief skirmish with the Natives on April 26. Percy would eventually become governor of the colony, and his tune would change in two and a half years after what he and the others were forced to endure.

Anyone who has visited Tidewater Virginia, especially along the James River, will admit that the springtime is truly lovely and temperate, with the breezes from the river fanning away any heat. But give the area a couple of months. When the breezes die and the humidity from the river settles in, it can be a tropical place.

The 104 settlers—all male—were tasked by their investors, the Virginia Company of London, to accomplish four things: establish a permanent English settlement; discover the gold which was said to exist in abundance in this new land; find the route west to the Orient, which everyone was convinced existed; and convert the Native peoples to Christianity.

They were told to look for ground, perhaps an island, where a large river narrowed its course for the natural defensive position it would afford against what would probably be Spanish attacks. Once they arrived in the bay, they sailed up the largest river emptying into it and named the river the James, honoring their king. After exploring all the way up to the confluence of what is now the Appomattox River, they sailed back and chose what became an island at high tide over another fine spot several miles downstream. They chose this location because the river was deep enough for the ships to tie up to the trees, facilitating unloading of supplies, especially the heavy cannon they thought they might need against the Spanish.

The island was vacant of any indigenous people and had a number of terrain features that would help in its defense. On May 14, 1607, the men disembarked onto their "island" and began to clear the land, create shelter, prepare rudimentary fortifications—what Percy called a "brush fort"—and post guards.

There were early attempts at peaceful coexistence when Indians from the nearest village brought news that their chief was arriving with a deer as a gift. Instead, the chief brought one hundred warriors as a show of power, but also "made signs" that the settlers may have as much land as they wished. Perhaps they misunderstood the signs? A warrior attempted to take a settler's hatchet, was struck for his efforts, and the Indians withdrew in a nasty mood. Thus would begin a series of costly military attacks and reprisals from both the English and the Natives that achieved little and added to the misery of both sides.

The Indians did eventually come back with the deer and a request to spend the night in the "fort." The request was wisely denied, and the settlers decided to demonstrate their weapons to prove to the Natives they were superior to arrows. The Indians left, but returned in a week, and on May 27, launched an attack with two hundred warriors. The battle lasted about an hour, killing a number of Natives and inflicting from eleven to seventeen casualties (depending upon the source) among the settlers. Two of their casualties died. The heavy artillery came in handy, finally breaking up the Indians' assault. Immediately, the settlers began to surround their encampment with a triangular palisade fort—one with upright log walls—completed after nineteen probably very nervous days.

During the construction, the settlers were sniped at by Indians in the swamp and woods nearby. One settler wandered off, was found shot by six arrows, and died in a week. As the heat rose during the summer, settlers who had brought armor and helmets discovered that the sun turned the metal into ovens. What provided excellent protection on relatively cool European battlefields was unwearable in the Virginia heat, found too time-consuming to put on during the sudden Indian attacks, and discarded, leaving the settlers more vulnerable to Indian arrows.

Their exertions building the fort, combined with rationed meals of wormy wheat and barley and foul river water to drink, took their toll. By June 25, only about ten of the men remained healthy enough to even stand. Twenty-five died in the following days of "bloody flux," "the swellings" (wounds inflicted by the Indians), and just plain star-vation. One man, believed to be a Spanish spy, was executed.

By the fall, according to Capt. John Smith, over seventy had died. But, by now, a young Powhatan princess came to the settlement every few days with food, which sustained the men. Her name was Pocahontas.

Not that the Indians had a lot to share during that period. Recent studies of growth rings of trees that were alive in 1607 indicates that the settlers just happened to land at the beginning of the worst drought in 770 years, which lasted from 1606 to 1612.

Right after the first of the next year, two ships carrying supplies and a hundred new male settlers docked at Jamestown Island. Shortly afterward, a fire destroyed much of the fort. Winter set in.

Capt. John Smith became manager of the settlement after the president had been caught hoarding food for himself, but Smith was also tasked with leading explorations of the Virginia coastline and its rivers. Things, according to him, seemed to fall apart whenever he was gone from the settlement. People quit work on improving their lot, got sick, let the crops rot—"all unable to do anything but complain."

Smith, with his military background and natural leadership abil-ities, got them back to work, restored discipline, and reorganized the militia, all the time drilling under the watchful eyes of the Indians who seemed impressed. With the next ships, two women arrived in Jamestown, along with some European craftsmen who created clap-board, wainscot, and samples of glass, pitch, tar, and soap-ashes to be sent back to England. Smith also established a "no work, no food" rule, which encouraged the uninspired to bend their backs to creat-ing salable goods, dig a sweet-water well within the fort, construct twenty houses, rebuild the church, weave fishing nets, and construct a defensive blockhouse at the neck of land connecting the island to the mainland.

The summer of 1609 saw them pull giant sturgeons from the river and plant tens of acres of corn, and, as Smith wrote, they "lived very well," which may have been more self-promotion than reality. Seven more ships from the mother country hove to at Jamestown, carrying supplies but also bringing something else: sedition. Instead of dropping off the supplies they carried, they actually took some from the settlers and sailed up the river to settlers at the Falls (near modern-day Richmond) and downriver to the Nansemond River. They also brought treachery: John Smith was ordered to be assassinated.

Come autumn, typically, Smith went after the miscreants upriver. He returned to Jamestown with a severe wound to his thigh, caused by an "accidental" firing of his bag of gunpowder. He needed surgery and none was available in the fort, and so returned to England. George Percy became president of the colony.

Smith recorded a list of all the provisions he left with the settlers, which should have lasted them ten weeks, as well as plenty of weapons, horses, pigs, goats, sheep, with the number of houses numbering about sixty. But he also forewarned about some of the men he left behind: "poor gentlemen, tradesmen, serving men, libertines ten times more fit to spoil a commonwealth than . . . help to maintain one."

In spite of the store of goods, with those men as part of its makeup, Jamestown was to face a combination of events that would drive them to the most desperate acts for survival.

Beginning in the summer of 1609, several of the supply ships sent from England were wrecked in Atlantic storms. Of those ships that did make it to the colony, historians speculate that one brought passengers infected with disease. During the winter of 1609–1610, the Indians laid siege to the fort so that nothing from the outside could get in, and the colonists soon consumed their stores of food. After the pigs, goats, and sheep, they began to kill and eat their horses; after that, their dogs and cats; then rats, snakes, and mice they caught; then their shoe and belt leather became food. Then, their own dead.

It becomes known as "the starving time," and George Percy wrote about it in his account of the colony. For a long time his story of cannibalism was thought to be some kind of hyperbole. This appears now to have been just wishful thinking on the part of historians. It goes against common sense: Who would take exaggeration far enough to condemn one's own people of such a heinous act? Recent archaeological discoveries at Jamestown by archaeologist William M. Kelso and detailed examination of the physical evidence has led scientists to conclude that Percy's account of cannibalism is true.

Although so far only one set of bones (those of a teenage female) has been discovered with obvious butchering marks upon the skull and leg bones, Percy writes that "nothing was spared to maintain life and to do those things which seem incredible as to dig up dead corpses out of graves and to eat them." Obviously writing in the plural indicates that it happened to more than just the dead teenage girl. His next entry is too detailed to ignore: "[O]ne of our colony murdered his [pregnant] wife, ripped the child out of her womb and threw it into the river, and after chopped the mother in pieces and salted [preserved] her for his food. The same not being discovered before he had eaten part thereof, for the which cruel and inhumane fact I ajudged him to be executed, the acknowledgement of the deed being enforced from him by torture having hung by the thumbs with weights at his feet a quarter of an hour before he would confess the same."

Again, who would admit to such awful acts if not for a dedication to tell the truth about Jamestown?

In spite of all their efforts—even the most abhorrent—only sixty of the settlers remained alive after the starving time.

The rest of Percy's account describes fights with Indians, kidnappings, their own colonists' hoarding food from each other, and a horrifying account of the capture of Captain Ratcliffe, who went to trade with Chief Powhatan: "[A]fter not keeping a proper and fitting court of guard, but suffering his men by two and three and small numbers in a company to straggle into the savages' houses when the sly old king [Powhatan] espied a fitting time, cut them all of [off], only surprised Captain Ratcliffe alive, who he caused to be bound unto a tree naked with a fire before, and by women his flesh was scrapped [scraped] from his bones with mussel shells and before his face thrown into the fire. And so for want of circumspection miserably perished."

But the Natives were not the only ones who could be cruel and unreasonable. Captain West decapitated two Indians and apparently cut off the limbs of others during an expedition to trade for maize.

By June of 1610, things had not gotten any better, and it was determined to abandon Jamestown. The colonists buried their weapons on the river side of the fort, and on June 7, sailed away from their dashed hopes and the graves of their fellow adventurers. Halfway down the James, however, they ran into the advance party for the resupply fleet, bringing their new governor. The provisions, munitions, and three hundred fit men Governor De La Warr brought were like a tonic. Within thirty hours they returned to Jamestown and began to prepare for their new governor's arrival.

In July, Humphrey Blunt was captured by the Indians and tortured to death.

In August of 1610, Percy was ordered on a punitive expedition against Chief Powhatan. They approached a town and attacked, killing fifteen or sixteen and running off the rest. They captured an Indian queen, her two children, and another male Indian and kidnapped them. Not wanting to be burdened with the man, Percy had him decapitated. He then burned down all the Indians' houses and destroyed their corn crop.

Percy writes about what happened next: "[M]y soldiers did begin to murmur because the queen and her children were spared. So upon the same a council being called it was agreed upon to put the children to death, the which was effected by throwing them overboard and shooting out their brains in the water, yet for all this cruelty the soldiers were not well pleased, and I had much to do to save the queen's life for that time."

They marched farther from the river and found another Indian town, burned their houses, cut down their corn, and apparently destroyed what Percy called a temple, a much larger building used for ceremonies, which was rare for the Indians to build.

On their way back to Jamestown, Percy's superior was not happy with him bringing the Indian queen along. Percy records what happened: "My Lord General not being well did lie ashipboard to whom we rowed, he being joyful of our safe return yet seemed to be discontent because the queen was spared, as Captain Davis told me, and that it was my Lord's pleasure that we should see her dispatched, the way he thought best to burn her. To the first I replied that having seen so much bloodshed that day now in my cold blood I desired to see no more and for to burn her I did not hold it fitting but either by shot or sword to give her a quicker dispatch. So turning myself from Captain Davis he did take the queen with two soldiers ashore and in the woods put her to the sword and although Captain Davis told me it was my Lord's direction yet I am persuaded to the contrary."

In spite of attacks and reprisals continuing through 1611, the English settlers expanded their presence up and down the James River. That year, an Englishman named John Rolfe arrived at Jamestown after being shipwrecked on Bermuda. With him he brought tobacco seeds, bootlegged from the Spanish.

Up until that time, the Spanish had held a monopoly on a sweeter tobacco grown in Trinidad. In fact, the penalty was death to anyone who would remove the seeds from the Spanish colony. Rolfe somehow sneaked some out and began cultivating the tobacco that was more in demand than the bitter tobacco native to the Virginia colonies. Interesting that those addicted to nicotine and its deleterious effects have called it a curse, but it was this product that helped to save the original English settlers in America. By 1612, Rolfe began exporting what would become the cash crop and savior of the colony in Virginia, and one of Virginia's main industries for the next four centuries.

In April of 1613, Pocahontas was kidnapped. But it seemed to turn out well when she met and married John Rolfe a year later. The union ended the first Anglo-Powhatan war, and the peace seemed to hold for a number of years. But the colonists kept coming. The Native Americans soon realized that their land was being usurped with each and every shipload, and that they were being driven farther west, out of their homelands.

Rolfe's tobacco crops had spread and helped to enrich settlements inland from Jamestown, but the cultivating of tobacco was labor-intensive. Indentured servants were introduced to the colony, and would eventually work out their indenture and be free of laboring for someone else. Then, almost accidentally, African slaves were brought in. John Rolfe recorded in 1619 that a passing Dutch ship, a man-of-war, on August 31 sold the settlers in Jamestown twenty Africans. They, however, would not be allowed to work their way to freedom, nor would their offspring for generations to come, until the nation fought a bloody civil war.

By March 21, 1622, settlers along the James River seemed to be prospering. The Indians had become so peaceful that the settlers allowed them into their homes. Then, on March 22, 1622, everything changed.

No one is quite sure to this day how the Indians managed the communication, but on March 22, all along the Tidewater area at virtually the same time, a massacre took place. The Indians, bringing in wild game to trade, took up the settlers' own tools—kitchen butcher knives, hatchets, axes used for chopping wood—and attacked the settlers. That day 347 settlers, men, women, and children—almost one-quarter of the entire population of Virginia—were slaughtered by the Indians. Of course, more reprisals would follow. And so it would go.

The curse of settlers fighting Native Americans that began almost on the very day that George Percy and the first ships full of Englishmen landed would continue nearly into the twentieth century.

2

YORKTOWN: A CURSE FOR THE BRITISH IN AMERICA

Americans often forget that while the Revolutionary War was taking place, we were all still British subjects. Many of us remained fiercely loyal to the British crown. And for the better part of the Revolution, it looked like the British were going to win.

Like in all wars, there were numerous arguments back and forth between military leaders, between politicians, and between citizens as to how the war should be won, whether you were for the upstart revolutionaries or loyal to your own country, Britain.

Britain, at the time of the American Revolution, was arguably the most powerful nation on the planet, with interests ranging from India to Canada, Africa to Bermuda, Jamaica, the Bahamas, and, of course, Scotland and Ireland. They were successfully fighting the other great superpowers, the Netherlands, France, and Spain, with their military might. They had the best army in the world and the largest and finest navy. By 1763, with the help of colonists in America, such as George Washington, they had won the Seven Years' War, also known as the French and Indian War. But it was incredibly costly, and they needed a new revenue (read: tax) source from which to relieve themselves of a budget deficit in excess of 122 million pounds. They decided to tax the colonists in America to obtain these funds.

Beginning with the Stamp Act of 1765, a series of taxes levied upon the American colonists helped precipitate talk of independence. The British felt it was only fair to tax the Americans for the protection provided by the British. Americans didn't see it that way, feeling that they lacked representation in the British government. Demonstrations, threats, and violence against British officials in America escalated. The Stamp Act was repealed in 1766, but the seeds had been sown.

Most Americans learn the history of the Boston Tea Party, the Boston Massacre, Lexington and Concord, and Bunker Hill, which was actually fought on Breed's Hill, and can remember some of the subsequent battles over the conflict that lasted more than six years: Fort Ticonderoga, the Battles for Long Island, Trenton, Monmouth, Germantown. Some of the military actions in the South are perhaps less well-known: Cowpens, Savannah, Charleston, King's Mountain, Guilford Court House. And we should emphasize the fact that the war did last over six years, because, in one important sense, the prolongation of the conflict was one of the deciding factors in the victory.

George Washington showed that he didn't have to win all the battles to win the war. It's probably a good thing, because militarily the Americans, which, at first, were merely militia, were no match for the veteran British Regulars who had seen combat on many continents over the years. Even up to the spring and summer of the last year of the war, American independence from Britain was still in the balance, with the scales leaning toward the British.

In January of 1781, Benedict Arnold, former patriot turned British officer, raided Washington's home state of Virginia, one of the wealthiest colonies in America, destroying grain mills, depots where supplies were stored, and other targets beneficial to the economy of Virginia. In February, Washington sent his young protégé, the Marquis de Lafayette, to the colony to stop Arnold. Without knowing it, Arnold had planted the roots of his newfound country's defeat in America.

By spring, Lafayette got word of the approach from the South of a much larger British army under Gen. Charles Cornwallis. He attempted to prevent Arnold and Cornwallis from uniting, but failed. At this point he was outnumbered, two to one.

A veteran general, Lord Cornwallis commanded a large, experienced British force. He was opposed by a tiny American army, led by the relatively inexperienced twenty-three-year-old Frenchman, Lafayette, who frankly admitted about his force, "I am not strong enough even to be beaten . . . Were I to fight, I should be cut to pieces." So, instead of directly engaging Cornwallis, he begged Washington for more troops and went on the run.

Cornwallis, amused by Lafayette's youth and tactics, bragged, "The boy cannot now escape me." But by rapid marches at night as well as day, he did just that, until joined by Anthony Wayne, whose troops had marched to Virginia from Pennsylvania. Now, with Wayne's troops, the hunted became the hunter; Lafayette turned on Cornwallis and pursued him to Richmond.

Lafayette was aided by the British plans to quarter in Williamsburg for the summer. The British considered the climate healthier for the troops than the swamps and woods farther west, and food supplies more plentiful. Now it was Cornwallis who was calling for reinforcements if he were to finish up the job in Virginia. Instead of sending them, his superior, Gen. Sir Henry Clinton, expecting an attack from Washington in New York, ordered Cornwallis to *relinquish* troops so that he might pursue his agenda against Washington in the North. Reluctantly, Cornwallis left Williamsburg and headed to Portsmouth to board troop transports for New York.

The Clinton/Cornwallis relationship is one of the reasons the Americans finally won their independence. The British strategy after 1778 was to split the colonies in two by subduing the southern colonies, where loyalist sentiment was high. Cornwallis successfully beat Americans at Camden under Gen. Horatio Gates, and won South Carolina. He marched into North Carolina where he pursued fast-moving Nathanael Greene's army. He fought him when he caught up and lost to Greene at Guilford Court House. Pondering his defeat, Cornwallis realized that Greene and his army were being supplied from Virginia. Rich Virginia was the key to the Southern states, a strategy he passed on to Clinton, and then awaited orders.

Clinton was living large in New York. One historian counted four houses available to Clinton, including a New York City mansion and a manor house out on Long Island. He had a mistress to keep him and his many guests happy. And he had his cronies to stroke his ego and reap military largess from it. According to one historian's estimate, Clinton spent, in the same amount of time as commander, three times as much of the King's money as his predecessor. But his communication skills were even worse than his greed.

Military orders should be short, precise directions. Clinton's letters (they can hardly be called official orders) to Cornwallis contained none of that. They allowed great discretion on the part of his subordinate (Cornwallis), and were frequently contradictory. His "orders" concerning Cornwallis's march to Portsmouth and debarkation to New York were typical.

Clinton suddenly reversed his orders to Cornwallis to come to New York, telling him instead to fortify Old Point Comfort on the James River at the extreme end of the Virginia Peninsula. Because the water was deeper, Cornwallis decided instead to locate his army farther up the Peninsula on the York River, where it narrows between Gloucester Point and Yorktown. By the end of August, 1781, Cornwallis's army of seven thousand was fortifying with trench works and redoubts the area around both places.

With the enemy ensconced in trenches on a river where, at any day, the British Navy with its mammoth cannon could arrive, Lafayette felt that he could not attack with his force. It was a stalemate.

In the North, Washington had only about four thousand troops to oppose Clinton's approximately eleven thousand, holding New York. There were another five thousand French allies under Comte de Rochambeau in Newport, Rhode Island, soon to march and join Washington. Though Washington wanted to attack, the odds were still against him. As were the circumstances.

Morale in the Continental Army was at an all-time low. The troops were on the verge of mutiny—in fact, had mutinied—only to be dissuaded by the grisly execution of the ringleaders. They had been promised pay for their services, but the Continental Congress in many cases reneged—not that it mattered, since they were paying in paper money which was virtually worthless. Washington's men were in threadbare uniforms, many barefoot, in need of weapons and ammunition and transportation for their measly rations. Beg as he might, Washington's pleas for his men were met with promises left unfulfilled. The hope for American independence, after six long years of frustrating warfare, seemed more distant than ever.

Then Washington learned of the approach of a large French naval force from the West Indies carrying reinforcements under Admiral de Grasse. They were to arrive near the mouth of the Chesapeake Bay in late summer. If Lafayette and Wayne could be reinforced, and Cornwallis denied reinforcements and supplies by bottling up the Bay . . .

But Washington was far from the York River and facing an enemy. He enlisted subterfuge as an ally. In plain sight of the British, he had his men build large brick ovens for baking bread, an obvious sign that they were in New York to stay. He also let his "plans" to attack Clinton slip into British hands. Convinced that Washington was going to attack him, Clinton hardly noticed when, in mid-August, Washington and Rochambeau, leaving a small force to face the British, slipped away and headed south.

By the end of August, Admiral de Grasse had landed some three thousand French reinforcements in Virginia to march to Williamsburg. On September 5, 1781, de Grasse's fleet, now blockading the entrance to the Chesapeake Bay, engaged the British fleet sent to reinforce Cornwallis. The British were defeated in what became known as the Battle of the Capes and returned to New York, leaving Cornwallis on his own.

By the end of September, Washington's combined forces of 17,600 surrounded Cornwallis's 8,300 men in their trenches. The Americans and French began digging siege lines around the British trenches about eight hundred yards away. On October 9, the allies had brought up their heavy artillery, and by October 11, after an almost continuous barrage, they silenced the British big guns. Cornwallis also learned that the reinforcements he had requested earlier from Clinton in New York had been delayed in their departure.

The night of October 11, with the British cannons out of commission, the French and American troops began a siege trench only four hundred yards from the British lines. The lines could not be completed, however, without the capture of two redoubts, or forts, within the British defensive line. Under the cover of night, on October 14, French infantry assaulted redoubt number 9, simultaneous with an American assault upon redoubt number 10. The fighting was with the bayonet, and vicious, but the redoubts were captured within thirty minutes.

On the morning of October 16, Cornwallis ordered an attack on the French artillery position in the center of the allied lines. Seemingly a success, it silenced the guns, but only temporarily. They were back firing again within six hours. That night after dark, the British began an amphibious withdrawal in small boats across the York, to Gloucester Point. As if even nature was against them, they got half their troops across when a tremendous storm broke and blew the rest back to the Yorktown side of the river.

With no reinforcements in sight, under constant barrage from the allied cannons, sickness running rampant in the ranks, and even the weather seemingly conspiring against him, Cornwallis made the decision, on October 17, to surrender.

On October 19, 1781, what was left of Cornwallis's army marched out of their siege lines between two lines of allied troops—one side American, the other French—to an open field and laid down their arms. On that same day, in New York, Clinton embarked five thousand troops on ships destined for Yorktown. They would never arrive. The ships got to the Capes five days after the surrender, turned around, and headed back to New York.

When the news hit both sides of the Atlantic, it stunned all who heard it. Most Americans were overjoyed; many British were also happy that the war with their American brothers was over. In fact, although many British troops were still in America and held vital terrain, war-weariness played a major role in the British decision to end the war and withdraw from the colonies.

In the six years the war lasted, it had taken on the aspects of a world war, with France and Spain taking the side of the Patriots, and the British still fighting in Gibraltar, the West Indies, India, and Ireland. The decision to replace Cornwallis's army was abandoned. The major British commanders were recalled, and spent much of their time arguing about who was to blame for the defeat. In 1782, Parliament passed a resolution to discontinue the war, and a formal treaty was signed in September of 1783, recognizing American independence.

And while historians can point to the fact that for six years, Britain was burdened with a three-thousand-mile-long supply route for men and materiel, others, pointing especially to the unwarranted foul-ups, mistakes, petty rivalries, and even the weather, will claim that some sort of supernatural event must have been in the stars to guarantee the existence of the United States of America.

3

BEAUTIFUL, QUAINT WILLIAMSBURG CURSED?

Today Williamsburg is known as the quaint, restored former colonial capital, drawing millions of visitors from all around the world each year.

Most people are unaware that for years it lay in the back of history's memory, a backwater byway, and pleased with itself to be that way. As well, most people don't know that it has a history woven around mysterious organizations, clandestine, nighttime archaeological digs, and one of the most celebrated scientists of all time.

Originally settled out of the forests of the Powhatan Confederacy, "Middle Plantation" became the home to William and Mary College, the second-oldest institution of higher education in America, in 1693. After the statehouse in Jamestown burned in 1698, students from the college petitioned successfully to have the colonial capital moved to Middle Plantation, which, in 1699, was renamed Williamsburg.

Between 1704 and 1722, Duke of Gloucester Street was straightened and made the main route through the village, the college expanded its number of buildings, and a church and magazine for arms and ammunition were constructed. A canal to connect the James and York Rivers was begun in 1771, but never completed. In the 1770s, the first psychiatric hospital in America was established in Williamsburg.

As the colonial capital, Williamsburg was home to the Royal Governor, but in 1775, all that changed. British Lord Dunmore, feeling the strong winds of American independence blowing, abandoned his post for his own and his family's safety. Subsequent elected governors after June 1776 revealed the sentiments of the new nation: Virginia patriots Patrick Henry and Thomas Jefferson served in the position as colonial governors.

When the British strategy in the American Revolution turned from the northern colonies to the southern in 1779, Williamsburg was abandoned as the capital in favor of Richmond, farther inland. On June 25, 1781, Lord Cornwallis and his army arrived in Williamsburg and spent more than a week there, until he received orders to march his troops to Portsmouth for departure to New York. His plans changed, and he entrenched his forces a few miles away at Yorktown to ensure a fateful rendezvous with the American and French coalition forces.

After his departure, Washington and Rochambeau arrived in Williamsburg. From there they marched to Yorktown, met with Lafayette, and in September and October of 1781, sealed Cornwallis in his Yorktown entrenchments, leading to his surrender and American independence.

After the Revolution, with the relocation of the capital, Williamsburg began a gradual decline. William and Mary lost some of its prestige with the advent of other major universities in America, and fires and the general economy took their toll. The capitol building burned in 1832, and the governor's palace fell into disrepair. Residents bitterly joked that when it rained, Duke of Gloucester Street was ninety feet wide and two feet deep. Another war for independence—this time, of the Southern states from the Union—brought distress to the residents of the sleepy former colonial capital.

In 1862, Williamsburg was in the path of an invading Union army as it marched up the Virginia Peninsula from Fort Monroe, "on to Richmond." Battles were fought in and around Williamsburg, and the buildings of the College of William and Mary served as hospitals for both sides. During the early twentieth century, Williamsburg became the center and showplace for restoration and archaeology, mostly funded by the Rockefellers. Today, as part of the "Historic Triangle" (including Yorktown and Jamestown), it is a major tourist attraction.

Through it all, Bruton Parish Episcopal Church has weathered the storms. Its original congregation, combined from other local congregations, coalesced in 1674, and once boasted as members such luminaries as George Washington, Thomas Jefferson, and James Monroe. The current church building dates to 1715, and has been in continual use since its construction. Serene and dignified as it is, the church and its adjunct graveyard harbor obscure yet fascinating tales involving a father of early science, the greatest playwright that ever lived, ancient mystical occult brotherhoods, and clandestine archaeological digs in the dark of night.

One enduring mystery involves seventeenth-century philosopher and writer Sir Francis Bacon and a secret vault allegedly buried in the graveyard of Bruton Parish Church, on the main street in Williamsburg.

Bacon was a founding member in 1606 of the Virginia Company, which funded the Jamestown settlement. In 1635, Bacon's half-brother Nathaniel arrived in America, and later allegedly buried numerous relics, as was Masonic custom, under the altar of the original church in Jamestown. His purpose was to hide and secure certain valuable—some allegedly priceless—documents seminal to the founding philosophy of the United States, as well as other rumored items important to ancient world history. The documents were eventually moved to Williamsburg and buried in a vault in the area that would become the graveyard for the Bruton Parish Church. Two twentieth-century researchers, Manly and Marie Hall, claimed to have discovered the site of the vault by deciphering codes hidden in some of Shakespeare's plays; an esoteric Elizabethan work, *A Collection of Emblems*, written in 1635 by George Wither; Francis Bacon's utopian novel, *The New Atlantis*; and ciphers on tombstones in the church cemetery.

The vault is allegedly made of brick, measures ten feet by ten feet, and is sunk twenty feet belowground. Some sources claim there is a tunnel that connects it to the George Wythe House nearby, a known hangout of early American patriots and authors of our founding documents, such as George Washington, George Mason, Benjamin Franklin, and Patrick Henry. The mystery is complicated by their connection to the Freemasons, the ancient, secretive brotherhood interwoven into the founding of the United States.

In 1938, an archaeological excavation was conducted where the vault was supposedly located, initiated by researcher Marie Hall. Historians were skeptical. How did she know where to dig? Using her and her husband Manly's research into ciphers hidden in Shakespeare's play *Hamlet*, Wither's work, and ciphers on tombstones in the cemetery, they easily located the foundation of an original Masonic Church in what is now the church cemetery. Could the vault have originally been located under the altar of that church?

For some reason, Bruton Parish halted the excavation before the vault was discovered. One must wonder: Were they getting too close to some occult truth?

Fast-forward to 1991.

On September 9, in the dead of night, a group of amateur archaeologists associated with an obscure church crept into the churchyard and began to dig. They did not find the vault that night, but their stated goals were met. They claimed their intent was to bring forward to the American people the spiritual legacy of the founders' philosophy that lay buried below our feet. This they did, at least locally. It became the Virginia State Story of the Year for 1991, and created a mini-revival of interest in the legend of the Bruton Parish Vault.

Just what occult mysteries still lie below the footsteps of thousands of unsuspecting tourists who wander between the graves of Bruton Parish Church?

Of course, it all relies on speculation, but is nevertheless interesting. Some of the items alleged to be contained in the vault are, of course, linked to Freemasonry. Some rumors even place Shakespeare's priceless original folios in the vault, as well as naming Sir Francis Bacon as the true author of his plays. Innuendo secures in the vault Bacon's visionary documents for America's "Utopian Democratic Commonwealth," as well as ancient documents of secret societies.

There may be maps leading to hidden covert writings of the early American patriots, and, most interestingly, to the locations of other vaults throughout the world. Fantasists speculate that the Bruton vault holds Bacon's birth records, revealing him to be the illegitimate son of "The Virgin Queen," Elizabeth I. Others go so far as to say it holds treasure from the Knights Templar, such as the Holy Grail or the Ark of the Covenant.

Until professional archaeologists and the administrators of Bruton Parish Church take seriously the four-hundred-year-old stories and more-recent archival and field research into the mystery of what lies under the graves—or whether anything lies there at all—we will all continue to wander through that cemetery, unaware of what treasures might be just a couple of yards beneath our feet.

4

THE CURSE OF
PIRACY AND
VIRGINIA'S MOST
FAMOUS PIRATE

According to the Virginia Institute of Marine Sciences at William
and Mary College, the Virginia shoreline, including non-tidal
and tidal bay shores, oceans, and inland bays and lagoons, covers an
incredible 10,577 miles. With all that wetted area available for cruising and hiding, it is no wonder that pirates found the Chesapeake Bay
a fine place to infiltrate.

Although pirates have existed for centuries, authors Mark P. Donnelly and Daniel Diehl in *Pirates of Virginia* call the fifty years from
1680 to 1730 "The Golden Age of Piracy," predominantly because the
practice was, in many instances, encouraged by governments. They
also document that it was the British who turned piracy into its highest (or lowest) form.

Considering that Britain is an island and developed seafaring as a
means to better British lives, it is no wonder that piracy was part of that
nation's seafaring adventures. Often fishermen plying the waters off
England and Wales would turn to the second, part-time job of piracy
should the opportunity present itself. During wartime, some would be
issued "letters of marque" by the government. Their job was to destroy
or disrupt the sea trade of an enemy country by capturing their ships
and cargoes. For this, they would be allowed to keep the spoils. The

government got what it wanted from the "privateers": an adjunct to its navy, free of charge. The privateers got what they wanted: riches far beyond what they might make in their own businesses.

When America became the so-called land of opportunity shortly after the founding of Jamestown in Virginia, piracy naturally followed. The English were wary of their military rivals, France, the Netherlands, and particularly Spain, who already had interests in the New World. As England tightened trade with new laws, Americans reacted typically: They rebelled, and by the 1650s American pirates and smugglers began to bloom.

Although potentially lucrative, the life expectancy of a pirate, according to Donnelly and Diehl, was only three to five years. Between disease, battle, and executions, few "retired" pirates existed.

One of the first settlers to embrace piracy once in America was William Claiborne. Arriving at Jamestown in 1621, on the same boat with future governor Sir Francis Wyatt, by the 1630s Claiborne was using his own privateers to resolve disputes around Kent Island, and on what is now known as the Eastern Shore of Maryland.

In the 1680s, three adventurers, Lionel Wafer, Edward Davis, and John Hingson, won a ship called *Batchelor's Delight* in a card game, bypassed the Spanish-controlled waters of the Caribbean as a suitable place to pursue their goal of becoming pirates, and sailed instead to the west coast of South and North America to ply their trade. They apparently accumulated a large treasure and, after King James II offered amnesty to pirates, headed toward England. On the journey they realized that the King's amnesty might not apply to them, so the crew drew lots to see where they would all go after splitting up. Davis, Wafer, and Hingson drew Virginia, but after establishing a plantation (named Batchelor's Delight, after their ship), they moved on, intending to settle in Norfolk.

Upon reaching Jamestown, they were arrested and told that the King's pardon did not apply in Virginia. The judge in the case was intimidated by the fact that pirates roamed virtually at will along the Virginia coast, and let the men rot in jail for three years before sending them to London for trial. The judge there let them cut a deal:

If they donated a portion of their booty to the Crown for a charitable cause, they could go free. The judge determined that since they had been captured in Virginia, and that Virginia had requested money to establish an institute for higher learning, King William and Queen Mary would donate the pirates' ill-gotten gains to create a college in Williamsburg, named, of course, William and Mary.

Other famous pirates plied the waters of Virginia's extensive coast. Captain Kidd accumulated other people's treasure and allegedly buried some of it along Virginia's shores before being hanged—twice, as the first rope broke—for his crimes.

Edward Teach, aka, "Blackbeard," one of the most famous and feared pirates of all time, was alleged to have been born in Accomack County, Virginia. His ship *Queen Anne's Revenge*, with forty cannons and a crew of three hundred, was a formidable force. Blackbeard, before going into battle to overcome a usually smaller ship, would braid his long black beard and intertwine fuses from his cannons in the braids. Lighting the fuses wreathed his face and head in a smoky haze. Bandoliers holding half a dozen loaded pistols and several bladed weapons completed his fearsome image. Sometimes just the recognition of his flag—a skeleton piercing a heart with a spear and toasting the devil with a drink—was enough to make another ship strike its colors and surrender. The celebrated pirate and his flotilla of ships was said to have hidden in an inlet near Smithfield.

With Blackbeard's antics along the Virginia coast, it wasn't long until he gained a nemesis in Virginia governor Alexander Spotswood. In November of 1718, Spotswood sent British naval officer Lt. Robert Maynard to track Blackbeard down and rid Virginia and the rest of America's coast of this pirate. In a short, fierce battle near Ocracoke Inlet, North Carolina, Blackbeard, head wreathed in smoke, fought hand to hand until he had received some twenty-five wounds, and succumbed. But the legendary pirate was too famous to die. His decapitated corpse, when thrown overboard, allegedly swam around the ship—three times—before being swallowed by the ocean. His head swung from the British ship's rigging as they returned to Virginia, carrying the survivors of Blackbeard's crew for trial in Williamsburg.

Convicted of piracy in March of 1719, thirteen were hanged along Capitol Landing Road. Others were executed and their bodies hung in chains to rot at Tindall's Point on the York River and at Urbanna on the Rappahannock as a warning to other would-be pirates. Their captain's slowly decomposing head swung on a pole where the James and Hampton Rivers merge; the spot is still known as Blackbeard's Point.

Eventually the skull was confiscated and became a silver drinking cup. Later, that was turned into the bottom of a large punch bowl named "the infant," used in Raleigh Tavern in Williamsburg for many years. Liquid refreshment was often consumed from it by some of America's most prominent founding fathers, usually left unnamed.

But without a doubt, the most famous pirate to ever visit the state of Virginia was John Paul Jones.

John Paul Jones, you say? Not *the* John Paul Jones, father of the United States Navy?

Yes. *That* John Paul Jones.

It is understood by all that he commanded a ship in the fledgling Continental Navy, but, like all Americans at the time, he was still considered a British citizen. At least by the British Crown. But how did he get to America? And how did he become a pirate?

He was born John Paul in Scotland, fourth of seven children. His oldest brother left home early, moved to America, married, and opened a tailor's shop in Fredericksburg, Virginia. When John was twelve he announced that he wanted to leave home and go to sea. He was apprenticed out for seven years on *Friendship*. One of his first voyages took him to Fredericksburg, and he visited his brother there.

His apprenticeship at sea took him to other more-exotic ports of call in the Chesapeake Bay region, back to England, and down to the West Indies. After a while, his master went bankrupt and John Paul was released from his servitude as apprentice. Perhaps it was the unsavory experience that affected him when he served for a time on a slaver. In no uncertain terms he expressed his feelings about the trade, calling it "abominable," and in 1772, got his own command. After killing the ringleader of a mutiny, he fled to America adding a new last name, "Jones," and naturally, he gravitated toward Fredericksburg. He also gravitated toward the lovely and well-to-do Dorothea Spotswood Dandridge, granddaughter of the famous governor. Probably much to the benefit of the future US Navy, she dumped him for the then current governor of Virginia, Patrick Henry. Whether Jones was in the gathering in the spring of 1775 to hear Henry request "liberty or death" is not known. In the fall, however, he traveled to Philadelphia to offer his knowledge of seamanship, navigation, tactics, and waterborne weaponry to the cause of American liberty.

His first shipboard experience under a seasoned captain fell far short of his expectations. In 1776 he was given his first independent command, *Providence*, and began sailing as a commerce raider—a privateer. According to a letter he wrote to a friend, in the course of just twelve weeks he captured twenty-four prizes.

But one country's privateer is another country's pirate. Still considered a British citizen by England, the Royal Navy became his enemy, with strangling at the end of a rope the potential fate if captured. In 1777 he advocated guerrilla tactics on the high seas, striking the British where they were most vulnerable and forcing them to assign ships to protect their own ports rather than attacking those in America. British-held ports in the Caribbean, Gulf of Mexico, and western Florida were targeted, but Jones was given another assignment in a new warship, *Ranger*: sail to Europe. There he, and the American navy, received the recognition of France. While there he engaged in capturing a British lord whom he intended to use to exchange for American sailors held captive, and defeated and captured a British warship. Some newspapers in England were by then calling him a pirate.

But his next encounter would prove he was much more than a mere privateer.

In the fall of 1779, aboard *Bonhomme Richard*, he engaged the fifty-gun British warship HMS *Serapis* off Flamborough Head in the North Sea, east of England. Realizing the great firepower of his enemy, Jones closed and grappled fast to *Serapis*. It became a hand-to-hand fight. British gunners blew holes clean through *Bonhomme Richard*. A misunderstood command brought the American flag down, and the British commander shouted through the din, asking if Jones wished to surrender.

"I have not yet begun to fight" were Jones's now-immortal words in reply. The heated battle lasted for over three hours, until an American grenade dropped belowdecks of *Serapis* exploded a powder supply and the British commander surrendered. Even after this decisive victory, many in Britain still considered Jones a mere pirate.

After the Revolutionary War, his adventuresome spirit led him to join the Russian Navy, where he fought battles for Empress Catherine II. In 1792, he died and was buried in Paris. Later, the cemetery was abandoned, and for a while his remains were lost. In 1905, using old maps, his remains were rediscovered and returned with full military honors to the United States he helped to create. He now lies in honor appropriately at the United States Naval Academy in Annapolis, Maryland.

5

THE CURSE OF
SLAVERY AND
SLAVE REBELLION

There are two dates in the history of Virginia that are largely ignored, yet mark two of the most crucial events in the state's—and America's—story.

On August 31, 1619, Dutch ships stopped by the twelve-year-old English colony of Jamestown brought the first few Africans to America and sold them as sort of an afterthought to the English colonists. They seemed to be all indentured servants with a time limit on their servitude.

One of the Africans who landed in Virginia in 1619 was an indentured servant named Anthony Johnson. After his indenture was up, he became a farmer, and bought some indentured servants himself to help work his farm. One of them, John Casor, demanded his freedom and received it, but then apparently indentured himself to another. Johnson sued the other black man who had purchased Casor's indenture and won the suit.

In 1653, Casor was returned to Johnson, but as a servant *for life*. It was a landmark case, and set precedent. It virtually "created" American slavery, although how Casor's progeny—or other blacks in Virginia—ended up servants for life is a mystery. One of the more surprising facts about this case is that all the main participants were black.

Shortly, ships from other countries, as well as the northern colonies of America, began to bring large, lucrative cargoes of humans from Africa and the West Indies to be sold to other Englishmen in America—both white and black, North and South—to toil without pay on their farms and in their shops. As the Industrial Revolution took hold in the North, a large labor force was not as vital to their commerce, and they sold their slaves farther south, to Southerners whose agrarian way of life demanded extensive human labor.

Thus began an institution that, once planted and established, grew like kudzu into every nook of American history. Although legally eradicated by the bloodletting of the Civil War, still to this day slavery and its moral ramifications poses some of the most heartrending challenges in American society.

And where there seemingly should be only one side to the analysis of American slavery, there are two. What should be recognized as an unmitigated evil is often equivocated upon, especially when one looks at it through the prism of the past.

For those of us of the twenty-first century, American slavery is an easy thing to condemn, as are those who participated in what has been called the "peculiar institution." Historians, however, point out that we are committing one of the major sins of the layman: seeing the past through our eyes of the present.

One generation's morals are not necessarily those of another; what is acceptable, even commendable in one era is not always proper or legal in another. Cultural equivalency over the decades doesn't exist.

For every enlightened member of Northern society that condemned slavery as a sin, there was one in Southern society who culled its condoning from a biblical passage. For every Northerner who expressed outright prejudice against African Americans, there was a Southerner who lived, worked, and associated with African Americans in their society.

So first you must realize that, for centuries prior to the Civil War, slavery was accepted in all the colonies, north and south. As well, it was accepted by both black and white slaveholding Americans. It was condoned for some 174 years while we were still colonies under the flag of Britain (and another 80-some years under the flag of the United States). Even the peace-loving Quakers of Philadelphia bought and owned slaves. And then we argued over, wrangled with, and tortured our national consciousness for another "four score and seven" years, until the most horrific ablution this country has known finally—allegedly—washed away the sins of the fathers. More than 620,000 Americans (some historians put the figure as high as 850,000) died during the four years of the Civil War—more American deaths than in all other American wars combined. It was a horribly high, unrecoverable price to pay for human freedom.

While it would be easy and sometimes fashionable to paint the entire Southern section of the country and its people with the same moral stain, history is never that easy—at least, for those who study it in detail. For every slave that was mistreated, there was one who was brought in as family; for every slave that lived a relatively easy life of a house servant, there were those who toiled and sweated to an early death in the hot fields. As slaves worked in the fields of the South, armed black men in uniform marched past to fight for their liberation. When slaves cowered, fearful of retribution for the smallest of infractions, incredibly courageous women like Harriet Tubman risked their own lives to lead them, in the dead of night, northward to freedom.

Like everything else in history, there is no one answer, no one cause. We are lucky if there is a simple duality.

Slaves sometimes took it upon themselves to fight for their freedom, and slave rebellions occurred periodically in the sections of the Americas and the world that supported slavery. Prior to the American Revolution, one of the largest slaveholding states was New York. In 1712, twenty-three slaves rose up in New York City, set a fire, and attacked those who responded to the blaze. Nine whites were gunned down or hacked to death with hatchets and swords. Seventy slaves, guilty or not, were arrested. Twenty-one were burned to death for shock value to other would-be insurrectionists. Fear of other slave revolts moved government officials to enact draconian laws. Punishable by death were the crimes of rape, theft, conspiracy, and property damage by slaves. The laws and punishments were apparently worth the risk for freedom, because in 1741, a series of suspicious fires again broke out in New York City, attributed to rebelling slaves. The legal proceedings were legal in name only: Neighbor accused neighbor, and it ended like something out of the Dark Ages, with the alleged guilty parties burned at the stake.

Richmond, Virginia's capital, became the focal point for Gabriel's Rebellion in 1800. He had grandiose plans after hearing of the success of the slave rebellion against the French that set up Haiti, the first black republic in the new world. Gabriel was betrayed by fellow slaves. Twenty-six of his followers, including Gabriel and two brothers, were hanged after an invasion that never really happened.

In Charleston, South Carolina, a slave who had purchased his own freedom, Denmark Vesey, was said to have organized a slave rebellion in 1820 by attempting to raise a slave army. His plan was complicated, involving capturing ships in the harbor for transport to Haiti, an attack on the local arsenal to obtain weapons, and the murder of slaveholders to free other "soldier" slaves. While word of the rebellion was being spread to the many slaves in Charleston, the news leaked to whites. No stockpiles of weapons were ever found, and plans for the rebellion proved vague at best, but Vesey and five others were arrested, tried, and executed by hanging in 1822.

Then, in 1831, in Southampton County, Virginia, perhaps the most important of the slave-led rebellions drew serious blood and created a tidal wave of emotion that would lead to American's mind-set for civil war.

Nat Turner was a child born in Virginia, on October 2, 1800. By all accounts he was a remarkable boy, and even at an early age displayed a high level of intelligence. As a youngster he played with other boys in the rural neighborhood, exploring local woods and fishing in the numerous ponds in that section of Virginia. He learned to read and write, according to some sources, all on his own. His parents praised his intelligence, and his playmates took advantage of it, having him lead them in their pranks. He also seemed to show an uncanny ability to recall things that happened before he was born, as confirmed by elders in the community. But by the time he was twelve years old, everything changed. Nat had been born a slave, and at that age he was separated from his white playmates and set to work around the farm of his owners, Benjamin and Elizabeth Turner.

As he grew up he was taught about religion, probably along with the Turner children, whose parents were Methodists, and it took a strong hold in Nat's heart. He grew so knowledgeable about religion that he was, in his early manhood, considered a lay preacher among his fellow slaves. Later he would earn the reputation of being something more, with powers bordering on the supernatural. Intensive studies of the Bible, fasting, and prayer led to Nat experiencing visions. Eventually the other slaves named him "The Prophet." As the years advanced, his visions grew in intensity, as did his awareness of the inherent unfairness of the institution of slavery.

Intelligent reasoning added to a religion-borne sense of right and wrong made Turner question what had always been accepted in his society: Why should some of God's earthly children be condemned to a life of backbreaking servitude while others enjoyed the fruits of their free labor? Why should one set of people be raised to lord over another set simply because of the color of their skin? And by what law, other than man's, should one person have total control over every aspect of another's life? Why not the other way around?

Nat, usually after fasting and praying, began to hear voices and have visions which he assumed issued from God. Once, when he had run away from his master after being flogged by a cruel overseer and was on the road to freedom, his fasting caused him to have a painful vision. In the vision he received a message that he must return and serve his earthly master. Upon voluntarily returning to his surprised master, he quoted biblical passages as to why.

Yet there may have been a more earthly reason why he returned. According to one biographer, he had apparently become involved on the Turner plantation with a female slave named Cherry. As if to defy the institution that enslaved them, African Americans like Nat and Cherry courted, worshipped together, sang and danced when their work was done, fell in love, married, and had children.

Then, in 1822, another blow struck. Nat and Cherry's master died, leaving a wife and minor children to run an entire farm. Nat's widowed owner could keep on three domestic servants; the other twenty slaves, Nat and Cherry included, would be sold off. Luckily—if anything about being a slave can be called lucky—they were not sold farther south, but to neighboring farmers. Nat went to Thomas Moore and Cherry to Giles Reese, close enough so they could maintain what could marginally be called a marriage, enough so that Cherry would bear at least two (and possibly three) of Nat's children.

Nat had known his new owner's wife Sally since they were children together, playing in the fields of her father's farm. She was a Francis, a familiar name in that part of Southampton County. Still, Nat's workload was hard, field-hand work, made more difficult by his knowledge and intelligence seething below the surface.

And he continued to have his visions, growing more and more lurid: "I saw white spirits and black spirits engaged in battle, and the sun was darkened . . . thunder rolled in the Heavens . . . blood flowed in the streams," he would declare later.

He conducted local "praise meetings," sharing the visions he continued to have, including seeing Christ with his arms spread as if on the cross, from east to west over Southampton County. On leaves he found figures of bloody men and numbers, drops of blood on the corn he was sent to harvest. Over the months, as he shared his visions, his "congregation" grew, drawn by the apocalyptic exhortations of the charismatic prophet.

A vision later convinced him that he was indeed ordained for a great God-directed purpose: a loud noise coming from the heavens, and the appearance of a spirit telling him to shoulder the yoke Christ had carried for the sins of men, and to "fight against the serpent," for now was the time the Bible foretold of, when the first should become the last and the last become first.

In 1828, Thomas Moore died, and because of the law of primogeniture, Nat became the legal property of Moore's son, who was nine years old.

To any adult man, white or black, to be bossed around by a child would be complete humiliation; to Nat, with his superior intelligence, it was beyond the pale. But a year later, Moore's widow remarried, to

Mr. Joseph Travis, who moved into Sally's house and became Nat's master in 1829. Travis was a wheelwright, and everyone expected him to make use of the most intelligent slave in Southampton County, train Nat as an apprentice, and perhaps even hire him out to make money off of him. Often, skilled slaves were given part of their earnings. Sometimes they saved enough to buy their own—and their relatives'—freedom. If that was what Nat thought would happen, he was disappointed. Travis worked his own wheelwright shop and Nat remained toiling in the fields, now waiting more than ever for a final sign to begin the task foretold to him.

Then, on February 11, 1831, Turner observed a solar eclipse. This, then, was the sign for which he had waited.

He began to gather to himself trusted fellow slaves to become "generals" in his slave army. They met at a place called Cabin Pond. Hark Travis, living with Nat at the Travis farm, was a physically imposing individual, called later a "black Apollo"; Nelson Williams, known as a sorcerer who said he could foretell the future; Sam Francis, who belonged to Sally Francis, Travis's younger brother; and Henry Porter. Nat and the others began to strategize, using a hand-drawn map created by Nat. They planned the execution date as July 4—Independence Day—for its obvious symbolism, but Nat fell ill at that time, and the insurrection was postponed.

Then an additional solar event on August 13 told Nat the time was ripe. Odd atmospheric conditions caused the sun to turn green, change colors to blue, then white. It was seen from South Carolina to New York. A dark spot soon appeared on its face, an omen, slaves in Southampton County believed. Nat Turner was convinced that now was the time. They met one last time on Sunday, August 21, 1831, at Cabin Pond to eat, drink, and make final plans. By this time the next day, they would be free men.

After midnight, in the darkness of early the next morning, Turner and his band began invading the homes of their masters, killing whole families using axes, hatchets, swords, and knives, so as not to alert their neighbors with gunshots. From farm to farm they went in the predawn hours, murdering slave owners and their families—including children—as they slept, and gathering—sometimes reluctantly—their newly freed slaves as part of their "Army," which eventually grew to around seventy men.

They first went to the farm of Joseph Travis. They bypassed Giles Reese's farm, possibly because Nat's wife and children lived there. Travis and Nat's childhood playmate Sally Francis Travis lay asleep in bed as Nat used a ladder to enter the house's second floor. He opened the front door for the others to enter. They wanted him to strike the first blow for their freedom. Nat swung his hatchet in the darkness and landed a glancing slash to Joseph Travis's head. Travis bolted up, screaming. Will, one of Nat's recruits who belonged to Sally's brother, stepped in and hacked the couple to death in their bed with an ax. Four other whites were found in the darkened house and similarly chopped into bloody pieces. Nat's masters were dead. He was finally free.

Some muskets were taken from the Travis farm. Outside, Nat drilled his followers as if they were militia. Someone recalled that the Travises had an infant; Will and Henry returned to the house and slaughtered the baby in its crib.

And so it went through the night. Down the road, Sal Francis came out of his one-room cabin (hardly a plantation manor house) and was cut down with axes and clubs. Mrs. Piety Reese and her son William were hacked to death. Their overseer was attacked but survived, maimed for life both physically and, no doubt, haunted mentally by what he had experienced.

Brandy stills were raided and the band moved on, well acquainted with the woods and back roads of this part of Southampton County. At Wiley Francis's farm, according to one source, some of his slaves formed a line and swore to fight the insurgents. Nat moved on, withdrawing his army rather than fighting other blacks; that was not his purpose.

Just before dawn, Nat and his army approached familiar ground. It was Elizabeth Turner's farm, where he had lived for much of his life. The insurgent band killed her overseer with gunfire. Once inside the house, Will axed Elizabeth, and Nat struck her neighbor,

Mrs. Newsom, who was visiting, with an old sword he had found. The blow did not kill her; Will stepped in and chopped her apart.

Nat tried to get his former fellow Turner slaves to come along; some did, but Davy Turner had to be threatened with death before he would reluctantly follow them.

By now there were fifteen in Nat's army. Some were mounted, and they split into two groups: those on foot led by Hark, and horsemen, led by Nat and Will.

Next for Nat was the widow Whitehead's place. Inside were Catherine and her pretty daughters Margaret and Harriet. Her son Richard, a Methodist preacher, was already outside working the fields. From the house the women saw the horsemen ride up to Richard, who spoke with them. Then they heard the group chanting, "Kill him! Kill him!" Will rained ax blows into Richard's body while he pleaded, "Why do you want to kill me?" After Richard was silenced, they turned to the house and watched as some inside, after what they had seen, fled into the fields.

Catherine had to be dragged out of the house, screaming and fighting, until Will all but decapitated her with his ax. Nat's men were roaming the house looking for whites, especially Catherine's daughters. One of her slaves, Old Hubbard, hid Harriet under a mattress and lied about her whereabouts when confronted by the axmen. Margaret had run outside and hidden under a cellar cap. Nat found her and she bolted until he caught up with her and pounded her to the ground with his sword. She was still alive until he took a fence rail and beat her to death with it. Some of the other Whitehead slaves had run off, and the others—fearing white reprisal, and shocked by the bloody violence they had just witnessed—refused to join Nat.

Hark and his band returned with the news: Henry Bryant and his family down the road were dead. Then the leaders of the insurrectionists strategized among the still-warm bodies at the Whitehead plantation and decided who should go where next, then split up again.

Nat's band approached Richard Porter's farm, but found it abandoned. The Porters had been warned by slaves of the approaching carnage. It seemed inconceivable to Nat that fellow slaves would not join him, and, in fact, help their white masters. But apparently the murder of unarmed men, women, and children was too much for some of them, the acts of either madmen or the hopelessly desperate.

Will took command of the horsemen while Nat went looking for Hark and the rest. As Will approached Nathaniel Francis's house, Francis himself was not there. Slaves had come from his sister Sally's with the news that there was an uprising going on, and all the whites were being killed. At first, Nathaniel thought it was impossible, but there was sincere fear in the slaves' account; he rode toward his sister's house to check on her. Also concerned, his mother went with him, leaving Nathaniel's wife, Lavinia, eight months pregnant, with his slaves, two young nephews, and Henry Doyle, the overseer.

The nephews were playing outside the house when Will's horsemen pounded up the dirt road. The three-year-old nephew ran out to greet them. Will cut his head off with his ax. The other nephew screamed at the sight of his brother's violent decapitation and gave away his whereabouts. The rebelling slaves swarmed him and chopped him up too.

The overseer ran from the house and was shot down. Will and another insurgent rushed the house and ran into Nelson, a Francis slave. He told them that Nathaniel and his mother had left, and Lavinia escaped to who knows where. He lied. He had hidden the pregnant woman in a cubby upstairs and saved her life. As the two rebels left the house, they came upon the local schoolteacher's wife, Mrs. Williams, frozen by fear and disbelief in the dirt road with her child. They chopped them down.

Some of the Francis slaves accompanied Will's band voluntarily; others had to be forced to come along. Back at the Francis farm, Lavinia emerged from her cubby to discover two slaves, believing their mistress dead or gone, fighting over her clothes. One of them attacked the pregnant woman with a knife but was stopped by another slave named Easter. Nelson got Lavinia out of the house. She found her mother-in-law with other women and children gathered on a nearby hill, fearing what the next minutes would bring. She and her mother-in-law decided to attempt to escape to the nearest town, Cross Keys.

Schoolteacher Williams ran into some black children on the road and they told him his family had been killed at the Francis place. Riding there, he discovered his headless child and wife hacked to death in the road. Out of his mind, he galloped southward toward North Carolina where he knew there was militia.

The mounted band swarmed over John Barrow, working the cotton field at his farm. He was a veteran of the War of 1812 and fought the insurgents hand to hand, but was outnumbered and had his throat slit.

By 9:30 a.m., the insurgency had grown to forty men, and all had horses. They had also found brandy and begun to imbibe. Nat spoke to them as a leader would, demanding discipline from his troops. One of the group challenged Nat, saying that the whites were too powerful and would soon respond to his foolishness. Nat countered with eloquence, and by saying the whites were outnumbered by the blacks in Southampton. If all the slaves rose, they would have their freedom.

They rode on toward the county seat, Jerusalem (now Courtland). By this time word had spread to the whites of the county. Couriers were sent out to raise the alarm with the militia, and dispatches were sent to Petersburg and Richmond. Southerners' worst fear had come true: A slave insurrection was under way.

Levi Waller's place was a somewhat self-contained settlement with a blacksmith forge and a wheelwright shop, his distillery, slave cabins, and even a boarding school taught by one William Crocker. The slow, sweltering midmorning torpor was shattered when word arrived at his place of a slave uprising against the whites, who were all being murdered. And they were on their way.

Waller sent word to the school, and the master and children came to his house where they thought they'd be safe. Before Waller had a chance to load the guns, the insurgents had galloped into the yard among the schoolchildren and begun beheading them. Waller hid and watched while they killed his wife and cut off the heads of his two daughters.

By now white militia had organized and begun to follow the trail of blood, which had not had enough time to soak into the earth. Most distressing was the sight at the Waller place: ten headless children, tossed in a bloody pile. One of the Waller slaves was found in the road, drunk. The militia cut his Achilles tendons so that he couldn't participate further in the rebellion. Another group of militia came upon him. That he was forever crippled wasn't enough. He was tied to a tree and filled with bullets, left as an example to other potential insurgents.

The backlash had begun.

It was nearing noon when the insurgents approached Jacob Williams's and Caswell Worrell's farms. An overseer was ridden down and disemboweled; Williams's wife and three children were killed; Worrell's family was murdered.

The widow Vaughan heard riders coming, and when they weren't who she was expecting, ran inside and bolted the door. She pleaded through the windowpane for mercy; an insurrectionist shot her in the face through the window. Her niece, a known beauty in the county, came down from upstairs and was shot and thrown into the yard, dead. The overseer and the widow's son were also killed.

At Bill Williams's house, the rebels killed him and his two children, found his wife, made her lie down next to her slaughtered husband, and shot her to death.

In the insurgent army, now numbering around seventy riders, including a few free blacks, discipline began to falter. Raiding brandy stills and the indiscriminate killing began to wear on the minds of the men. Some had not killed anyone. Slaves who had been brought along against their will started to drift away. Nat headed the column toward Jerusalem. There he believed he would find modern arms and rally more slaves to his cause.

About two miles from Jerusalem they spied a party of mounted men on the road to James Parker's. It was about eighteen white men, all armed, who had answered the first warnings of a slave rebellion. Now Nat could command his men in a real battle. He ordered them to charge the enemy and broke and scattered the whites' line. Victory! And freedom for the black man was within sight. But then white reinforcements arrived and attacked, wounding five insurgents. Nat collected his wounded and ordered a retreat into the woods he and his men knew so well. Still, he planned to attack the county seat.

White militia, however, swarmed near Jerusalem, so Nat decided to head south to raid more white farms and gather more slave-soldiers. But the word had spread. The farms he found were deserted, including the farm of Mrs. John Thomas, who had fled with her son George. In one of those bizarre happenstances that only history can provide, it was, without a doubt, a good thing. He was destined to play a role in the successful liberation of Nat Turner's people in the bitter Civil War to come: Future Union general, Virginian George H. Thomas, "The Rock of Chickamauga," was evacuated before the slave insurrection could find and kill him.

Nat encamped his "army," now down to forty men, for the night. Meanwhile, whites were mobilizing. Word of the rebellion had reached Richmond, and state militia units were marching. Rumors, fed by fear, flew. Norfolk and Portsmouth militias mobilized. Ironically, federal troops from Fort Monroe, from the US government, were called out to quell the slaves. North Carolina, right across the state line, also panicked, and volunteers gathered to stop what they thought was coming their way.

Uncertainty invaded Nat's camp that night as well, and more of his slave army deserted. He was left with only twenty stalwarts. Near dawn they rode to Dr. Blunt's house to see if they could get reinforcements from his sixty-some slaves. When Hark fired his musket to awaken those in the sleeping household, he drew a volley from the house, killing one and wounding several others, including Hark. As Nat's men reeled, they were charged by Blunt's slaves, armed with clubs and farm implements.

It was disheartening, perhaps even incomprehensible to Nat—that slaves would fight against their own liberation.

Still following Nat, the hard-core members of his slave rebellion ran into more militia who fired upon them, killing three more, including Will, who had done so much killing himself. Now, Nat's army consisted of only four.

He sent two of them south to recruit more slaves. They went reluctantly, and were captured and taken to Cross Keys, where other blacks—perhaps insurgents, perhaps not—were being held. Nathaniel and Lavinia Francis had a happy reunion there. Easter, the slave who had saved his wife from the knife attack, was there, too, and embraced by Nathaniel. Charlotte, the slave who had tried to kill Lavinia when she found her still alive, as the story goes, was found by Nathaniel. Out of his mind with anger, he tied her to a tree outside and shot her to death, an inkling of the white backlash that was to come.

Nat and his two final followers were hiding in the familiar woods near the Travis place. He sent them as scouts to find the other leaders; they would rendezvous at Cabin Pond, where it all had started a day and a half ago. When they didn't return, Nat stole some provisions from one of the farmhouses he had forced the whites to abandon, found a pile of fence rails, and dug himself a cave in which to hide, until . . .

White militia and US troops flooded the county. Rumor had put the insurrectionist army at over a thousand. What was not rumor was the horror described by the white survivors. Retribution was in order, some cried. And blacks in Southampton County, whether associated with Nat Turner's rebellion or not, were hunted down.

Perhaps most confusing to the whites were the free blacks who had chosen to participate: Billy Artis, Benjamin and Thomas Haithcock, and three unnamed boys. Why would they, free already, risk everything to free others? The answer, to this day, has the sweet smell of the sublime. Thomas and some of the boys were captured. Artis was found, his hat hung up, a pistol next to him. He had made the choice: No white man would ever kill him.

Fear took over in Virginia. A Southerner's worst nightmare was the specter of thousands of blacks who had access to the outnumbered whites, twenty-four/seven, as well as all the whites' belongings, including weapons, to rise up.

Driving the response to the insurrection as well was outright racial prejudice. The hue of one's skin was enough to determine life or death.

Some local vigilantes took the law into their own hands and went wild, killing blacks where they found them. Others, driven by pure racial hatred, invaded the county just to kill blacks. An organized cavalry unit from North Carolina rode into the county and killed some forty blacks in forty-eight hours, beheading fifteen and placing the heads on pikes "as a warning."

At Cross Keys, five blacks were lynched, others were tortured, burned to death, and had their bodies mutilated in ways so hideous that witnesses were loath to describe them. One historian places the body count at 120 blacks murdered, and probably more. Nat's Cherry was found and whipped until she gave up his papers. Even with this "evidence," no more could be discerned about the Prophet, as Nat was called, since it appeared to be random numbers, strange signs, and rantings known only to him.

On August 31, 1831, the trials began without Nat, who had vanished into the Southampton woods he knew so well. Guilt or innocence of charges of treason, conspiracy, and insurrection was decided by a number of governor-appointed justices, not a jury. Fear-driven retribution and the desire to show future would-be insurrectionists their fate indicated to the justices what their verdicts should be. Still, the governor and justices felt an obligation to show that the system was fair, even to insurrectionists. One check to mass executions was the fact that for every slave put to death, the master/owner must be compensated by the State of Virginia for that slave's worth. The state couldn't afford that. Three attorneys risked social ostracism and defended the blacks.

Hark and other leaders of the rebellion were tried on September 3, found guilty, and sentenced to hang, with appropriate compensation to their owners. Nat was still nowhere to be found.

But his reputation was. Whites' imaginations, fueled by desperate fear and unsubstantiated newspaper reports, had him leading a slave insurrection in North Carolina, and innocent blacks were slaughtered there until it was proven to be a rumor.

Nat was said to be gone from the county. Then it was said that he had been spotted near where the slaughtering of whites had taken place. In fact, he had been moving at night through the area he was most familiar with, and had apparently considered surrendering. He had abandoned his old "cave"—the hole dug under fence rails—and had constructed a new one under a fallen tree. Patrols had just passed by on October 30, 1831. Nat started to emerge from his hideout only to stare into the barrel of the shotgun of Benjamin Phipps, who was about to become quite rich with the thousand-dollar bounty on Nat's head.

All along the route to Jerusalem, mobs lined the road to get a glimpse of the Prophet. Perhaps they were surprised. He was not a big man, around five feet, seven or eight inches, and his weeks on the run had turned him into a virtual skeleton. But his demeanor, perhaps, was what infuriated them most. He held his head high. When they whipped him once, just to please the crowd, he smiled. When they clamored for his lynching, he was resolute and unrepentant. Before the justices in Jerusalem, he spoke freely and admitted that he was the sole leader of the rebellion, related his revelations from God, and the signs he finally saw that had caused the rebellion to begin.

On November 1, attorney Thomas Gray entered Nat's cell and began to take down the dictated "confession" of Nat Turner. The Prophet took two days to complete his "confession." Though some have discredited the statement as coming from the imagination of a slaveholding white Southern male, historian Stephen B. Oates, in his short but comprehensive work, *The Fires of Jubilee: Nat Turner's Fierce Rebellion*, with the exception of a few obvious inclusions by Gray, indicates that Nat's confession goes along with what he had told the court a few days before. While other contemporary writers tried to paint Turner as a coward, sorry for the deaths he had caused, Gray came away with the impression—and so wrote—of Nat's bravery, commitment to his cause, and zeal, which he needed in order that lives be taken.

On November 5, the trial of the Prophet began. Authorities did everything in their power to prevent this from being a lynching. But the judge was a slaveholder himself. Nat pleaded not guilty, because that was the way he saw it. God had guided him in his endeavors to free human beings, so how could he be guilty? The State did not see it that way. There was no evidence, nor were there any witnesses presented by the defense. He was found guilty and sentenced to be hanged.

On November 11, 1831, he was taken to the old tree that was used as a gallows. Asked if he wanted to say anything to the large crowd that had gathered, he said he did not. "I'm ready," he said. The noose went around his neck. It was as if he was already gone. They pulled him up off the ground, but he didn't struggle or move a muscle, as determined in death as he had been in life. As to his body, one historian stated that they skinned it and made grease from the flesh.

Nat Turner's legacy haunted the South for the next thirty years. After Nat's bloody insurrection, every loose shutter flapping in the wind at night across the Southland became an enraged slave army breaking into a house. Paranoia ate at generations of Southerners as stories were passed down of the horrors slaves were capable of inflicting upon whites at the drop of a hat. As well, in 1831, William Lloyd Garrison began publishing *The Liberator*, a newspaper whose very theme was the abolition of slavery. Garrison's abolitionist writings eventually included condemnation of Southerners as sinners for holding slaves, and abolitionist societies throughout the North loudly calling for the destruction of a way of life followed by generations of Southerners.

Slavery was political in the sense that fear of losing power—and votes—drove politicians to demand, during the expansion of the United States, that a slave state be allowed to enter the Union for every free state. Because there was a physical limit to expansion, it was an untenable situation.

Then came John Brown, who, just twenty-eight years after Nat Turner, led another failed slave insurrection by capturing a federal arsenal at Harpers Ferry, Virginia, hoping to arm the slaves. He too was hanged, and became a martyr to the abolitionists, who ramped up their demands. He also rekindled the constant, nagging fear among white Southerners of being killed in the night by slaves with whom they worked during the day.

After the election of Abraham Lincoln—who, despite his public pronouncements, was seen by Southerners (among other things) as a "black republican," antislavery president—the Southern states began to secede from the United States. The American Civil War ensued, and Virginia, as the virtual seat of war, would be cursed by it.

6

THE CURSE OF
BALL'S BLUFF

After the Civil War Battle of First Manassas in July of 1861, the two armies settled in Northern Virginia, with the Potomac River as the demarcation line. The country had not seen such carnage as was wrought by the battle since the Revolution, two generations past. Both sides suddenly realized that this may not be the quick, easy war each had predicted. Winter was traditionally a time of rest and refitting for mid-nineteenth-century combatants, and so Maj. Gen. Joseph E. Johnston, commander of the Confederate forces, and Maj. Gen. George B. McClellan, head of the Union Army of the Potomac, were reluctant to plan any major military activity until spring. Of course, neither knew the other's plan.

McClellan, as his later actions would prove, was paranoid about the enemy, continuously overestimating his opponent's numerical strength and armaments. He sent a constant barrage of requests to President Lincoln for additional troops, and was never satisfied with the strength of his forces, using it as an excuse for dragging his feet when it came to taking the offensive. Yet, he occupied his troops' time between battles to drill and organize them into a well-tuned fighting force.

Johnston, as concerned about McClellan's intentions as McClellan was about his, was the first to act, pulling his troops farther away from Washington and closer to Centreville. McClellan then occupied the former Confederate positions across the Potomac from Washington.

But some thirty-five miles up the Potomac was a small Confederate force at Leesburg. McClellan believed that it would take just a minor demonstration to push the Rebels back from that section of the river and secure a large part of Northern Virginia for the Union.

Across the river from Leesburg, three Union infantry brigades under Brig. Gen. Charles Stone, which he somewhat pretentiously named "The Corps of Observation," watched the Confederates there.

Stone was from a military family and had graduated himself from West Point. He'd fought in the Mexican War, and was one of the first to volunteer when the tumultuous year of 1861 rolled around. Amid numerous rumors about attempts upon Lincoln's life before the inauguration, Stone was instrumental in getting the president-elect through Baltimore and Washington to his swearing-in. He had guards posted at all the roads and bridges into Washington, and even stationed guards at the normally wide-open Executive Mansion—the president's home (now called the White House). He had even personally ridden with the mounted guard for Lincoln's carriage that transported dignitaries to the inauguration, including one of Lincoln's closest friends, Senator Edward "Ned" Baker. By all accounts Stone was an up-and-coming officer. There would come a time when he'd wish he'd never heard of Leesburg or the cliffs on the Potomac nearby, named Ball's Bluff.

Abraham Lincoln as well, within the year, would also regret ever hearing of Ball's Bluff.

The Rebels in Leesburg were commanded by Col. Nathan Evans, who had distinguished himself at Manassas. He was the one who ascertained that the Union advance upon the stone bridge at Manassas was a mere feint, and acted quickly when he received E. P. Alexander's semaphore message that his left was in danger. Yet he was not as highly regarded as Stone. Perhaps it was because of his personality—"rip-roaring, scorn-all-care," according to a fellow officer. He also drank, some thought too much, in an era when it didn't take much to be labeled. At Manassas, Thomas J. "Stonewall" Jackson received accolades (and a legendary nickname) for remaining in position; Evans, for taking an active part in saving the Confederate army there, received little or no recognition, except from historians who cannot bestow advancements in rank. Advancement for Evans would come later, as would condemnation for his drinking. At Leesburg and in the coming fight, he would prove that he was not only a fine outpost officer, but reaffirm his battle credentials. Between the town and the river his troops had constructed a small fort, dug from the earth, and named it "Fort Evans," after their commander.

The nature of the ground between Leesburg and the Potomac would have as much to do with the results of the battle there as any command decision made by the officers in charge. At the edge of the river was a "bluff," or steep cliff, between eighty and a hundred feet high leading down to the water. At the top was an eight-acre open field, with only dirt pathways and farmers' fences, reached from the river by winding cow paths. In the middle of the river was five-hundred-acre Harrison's Island, blocking direct water access for three miles from the Maryland shore to the Virginia shore.

At the urging of McClellan, in the third week of October Gen. Stone ordered demonstrations to determine the Confederate presence in Leesburg. On the night of October 20, 1861, twenty men from the 15th Massachusetts set out to cross the Potomac and scout Confederate positions at the bluff named for a local family. Because of the sheer ruggedness of Ball's Bluff, it was thought to have been left unguarded by the Rebels.

An advance across the river at that point involved two amphibious landings. First the party must cross on waterborne conveyances to Harrison's Island, traverse the island, then cross to the Virginia shore. So it is understandable that the scouting party took several hours before reaching Ball's Bluff. Once atop the cliffs, they advanced to within two miles of Leesburg. There they stopped. Ahead, in the moonlight, they saw what they thought were about thirty tents of an encampment. Upon returning to Harrison's Island, Capt. Chase Philbrick reported what he had seen to his commander, Col. Charles Devens. Receiving the intelligence, Stone ordered Devens to cross the river and destroy the Confederate camp.

Devens's troops fought against the current of a river swollen by recent rains. Only three boats could be found on Harrison Island—

fine for sending a small scouting party across, but not so for any larger force, like the approximately three hundred with Devens. Even though they started for the Virginia shore at midnight, it was about 4:30 a.m. when they all reached the point below the Bluff.

When they got to the spot where Philbrick said the tents were pitched, they realized that there was no encampment. The young officer had not further investigated what he'd seen from a distance. The tents turned out to be a line of trees on the ridge, or some historians say, haystacks. Word was sent back to headquarters relaying what they had found.

Stone, after receiving this information, may have deduced that the Rebels had withdrawn and that his troops could stay in Virginia, at least long enough to find out more about the Confederate whereabouts. He made arrangements to provide a diversion, if Confederates should appear, so that his troops could withdraw, and ordered a unit to a spot on the Virginia shore to secure Smart's Mill, to which his Virginia force could retreat, re-crossing the river at a low-water ford without having to maneuver over a bluff or needing boats. As well, he placed Col. Edward Baker in command of the entire force across the river in Virginia. He was the same Senator Baker, Lincoln's good friend "Ned," whom Stone had protected in Lincoln's carriage en route to the inauguration.

How Baker became Lincoln's friend and had arrived on the Potomac across from Leesburg and Ball's Bluff is an interesting story. Born in England in 1811, his parents moved to America when he was only four years old. At nineteen he had become a lawyer, by twenty, married, and moved to Illinois. In 1835 he had settled in Springfield, where he practiced law and met another young lawyer, Abraham Lincoln, and was elected to the state senate. Before he moved to Springfield he had served as an officer in the Black Hawk War, then later in the Mexican War, where he was wounded twice. Elected to Congress in 1848, he drew the admiration of fellow congressmen, including his old friend, Abraham Lincoln. After his term he moved to California to practice law, and in 1860 moved to Oregon and was elected US senator from that state. Back in Washington, he witnessed his friend from Springfield inaugurated sixteenth president, and remained a staunch supporter of Lincoln's policies. When the war broke out, at fifty years old he volunteered. The law disallowed any sitting member of Congress from becoming a general officer in the military. Although offered a generalship, he instead accepted a colonelcy, and remained in the Senate. In time he commanded the 71st Pennsylvania Regiment from Philadelphia.

On the morning of October 21, 1861, Baker found himself subordinate to General Stone, receiving the command of a large reconnaissance force moving into Rebel territory. Baker had his orders from Stone to ascertain whether a strong display of Federal troops might force the Rebels back from Leesburg. If that happened, Baker was not to pursue too far; Confederate reinforcements could be sent to the withdrawing Rebels and threaten Baker's movement. How Baker interpreted these orders seems to have been different from his commander's intent.

In the meantime, fighting had flared in the field at the top of Ball's Bluff. Devens, like most officers of that war, was reluctant to yield ground until absolutely necessary. Lt. Church Howe, a quartermaster who had come across the river before dawn with the 15th Massachusetts, became an inadvertent instrument in the conduct of the battle as a courier of news from the front to the commanders in the rear. He was ordered to report to General Stone, to inform him of the battle going on beyond Ball's Bluff. At Harrison Island he ran into Lt. Col. George Ward, who had been ordered to secure the Smart's Mill Ford, the escape route if things went bad for the Union. Apparently Howe's narrative conveyed impending doom for the forces under Devens, and Ward abandoned his current mission to secure the ford and began to cross his men to the foot of the Bluff and assist Devens.

Once on the Maryland shore, Howe ran into Colonel Baker on the towpath of the Chesapeake and Ohio Canal and informed him of his impression of potential catastrophe for Devens. Baker responded by galloping off toward the battle, saying he was taking his entire force. Howe then continued to Stone's headquarters and told him what he had seen and what the two commanders he had run into were doing with their troops. Stone responded by noting that Baker was in charge now and will "arrange things to suit himself." Stone effectively removed himself from command.

By the time Howe returned to the battlefield around noon, Devens had been attacked by Confederate cavalry. He told Devens that Baker was now in command but had no specific orders from him. Devens assumed that meant he was to hold his ground, but Baker could not be found to clarify.

Howe was sent to find him. Instead he found more Union troops crossing over to the Virginia side. Union cavalry reported to the wrong officer and were sent back to the Maryland shore when they might have been used in the battle. Thus was the confusion growing without a commander on-site.

Finally Baker was heard from. He had the six hundred men from his Pennsylvania regiment put into motion with orders from Baker to their commander to find anything that could float and get all the men across to Virginia. Baker, however, was still on Harrison's Island, not yet having personally reconnoitered the battlefield above.

Now the battle seemed to take on a life of its own. Confederates engaged called for more troops; Federal forces were now rapidly approaching the fighting. By 12:30 p.m. Confederates bloodied Devens's force, and he withdrew closer to the Bluff where more Federal troops had been placed. There was a lull in the fighting as troops from both sides arrived on the field and fell into formation. Still, Colonel Baker was not on the field.

Instead of getting to the field of battle to see what was going on, Baker was on Harrison's Island, attempting to locate more boats. He apparently spent more than an hour himself supervising the moving of a canal boat to the river. For some reason, he felt it was important for him to do the work of a subordinate officer instead of directing the battle going on above him on the Bluff. Troops were still clogged up on Harrison's Island.

But the Confederates were also having organizational problems. One regiment was running out of ammunition. Word was sent back to Colonel Evans, who replied that the men should just "fight on."

Later another request came in for ammo and Evans sent back word they should hold their ground until "every damned man falls." He was later accused of already having had too much to drink. Yet Evans was sober enough to realize the precarious situation and send more troops to the field at the double-quick.

By 2:15 p.m., Baker finally made it to the battlefield, and, without personal reconnaissance, began to orchestrate his troops into strange formations, some of them into an "L"-shaped line. But the real problem was that his formation had no depth; there was no room for reserves, with the Bluff only fifteen feet behind them. Devens was pleased that Baker had finally made it to the field, absolving him of the responsibility. Baker seemed happy with the disposition of his troops, even taking time to quote poetry. Only one officer suggested that the line was vulnerable at a certain point, and he was ignored by Baker. Firing soon broke out, and the folly of the tactical arrangements for the Federals would soon be evident.

The Confederate line formed a semicircle around the Federals, naturally flanking them. Though the Union commanders launched assaults to stop this infiltration, they were hampered by the lack of space in which to maneuver. As the Rebels pressed them, some of the officers realized their predicament: There was nowhere to go except over the cliff to their rear; then where? It took hours to shuttle the men across from Harrison's Island on the seven boats that could be found. In an emergency, a full-scale retreat, how could they get back?

Around 4:30 p.m. an event that would affect how the rest of the war would be fought occurred. Colonel Baker was walking in front of his lines, observing the battle, when a body of Confederates rushed out of the woods to his front. According to eyewitnesses, a large, red-headed Confederate in his shirtsleeves emptied his revolver into Baker, killing him instantly. There ensued a battle between the two sides over Baker's lifeless body, which the Federals won. The redhead was killed in the fight and Baker's body was carried from the field, down the cow path along Ball's Bluff, and into a flatboat filled with wounded being evacuated. Now things began falling apart fast for the Federals.

On the battlefield, no one knew who was in command. Strategy as to extricating the men from this battle differed. One officer wanted them to fight their way through the Confederate lines to safety. Their charge was broken by the Confederate line. Weird stories began to circulate that the charge was led by a Confederate as a ruse, to bring the Federals into a trap; since no one was able to identify the officer, others believed a bizarre rumor that it was a phantom from the spirit world, leading the invading Yankees to their doom. Later, a Federal officer admitted that he had led the charge, but good ghost stories die hard. The battlefield is allegedly haunted today by the phantom officer, as well as the disgruntled spirits of those sacrificed there.

The sun was setting and the battlefield of Ball's Bluff was indeed beginning to take on an eerie demeanor, which is why when one officer ordered his men to withdraw to the "ferry," the order was quickly passed along and repeated. With the river so close, albeit a hundred feet down, it didn't take long for the retreat to turn into a rout.

Men ignored the option of evacuating single file down the cow path and began rushing headlong down the bluff. Some stumbled and fell, cartwheeling down the slope. Others leapt into the growing darkness and landed upon their comrades, breaking limbs and crushing skulls on the jagged rocks below. Once they got to the riverbank, there was no place to go. The few boats they had were overflowing with wounded. As the boats left the bank, men waded into the water and tried to climb in, capsizing the already overloaded vessels and sending the helpless wounded into the swift current to drown. Some decided they could swim the fifty feet to Harrison's Island. They took off their coats, but their wool pants and jackets soon absorbed enough of the Potomac to drag them down.

Those who still floated faced another danger. Confederates were now at the top of the bluff and began firing down at the Federal masses huddled on the shore—an easy target. As well, they plunked away at the hundreds of heads bobbing in the river. One witness said the surface of the water turned white as in a hailstorm from the bullets' impact. Some of the men were reluctant to discard their muskets and tried to swim with them—an impossible task. Officers especially attempted to take their swords with them, and either ended up dropping them in the river, or drowning with them. Men attempted to swim with their money; an officer whose body was found washed up by a Confederate had $126 in gold in a pocket that had weighed him down to his death.

Some men scavenged any kind of floatable device they could find: a piece of board for a raft; a tree limb; a floor joist from an abandoned building. Some who'd made it to the island built a ferry/raft out of fence rails fastened together with army belts to shuttle comrades to the island from Virginia. Just as the "pilot" was returning to the island with three men aboard, the belts broke and the raft fell apart. Two men disappeared below the surface of the Potomac.

The few small boats were ferried back and forth across the Potomac numerous times through the growing darkness, but many of the Union soldiers left on the Virginia side for too long were captured, to be sent to Confederate prisons. Other than rounding up prisoners, the Confederates apparently had had enough fighting for one day. They retreated back to Leesburg and Fort Evans, leaving a handful of pickets to watch the river.

Word of Baker's death reached Lincoln and the message hit him like a blow. He staggered unsteadily for a moment, his large hands clutching his chest. Once in the street it was feared he would fall, but he recovered and made it back to the Executive Mansion. To understand how close he and his family were to Baker, it must be remembered that the Lincolns' second son, who had died in 1850, had been named Edward Baker Lincoln, after his old friend.

The Battle of Ball's Bluff involved about 3,300 men about evenly split between both sides. Casualties as reported in the Official Records were a little higher on the Union side, with 49 killed to 36 killed for the Confederates, and 158 wounded to 117 wounded for the Confederates. Other sources place the Union dead at 119 and higher. The real discrepancy comes in the figures for the missing. According to the Official Records, the Confederates had only 2 men missing; the Union reported 714 missing.

Many of those Union soldiers were captured; Confederate colonel Evans reported that he sent 529 prisoners south, and added 24 in

Leesburg too badly wounded to travel. The battle was over, but the horror was about to begin.

Within two weeks, bodies began to arrive in Washington via the muddy waters of the Potomac. Five bodies were pulled from the water near the Chain Bridge, mutilated by their journey; others were caught in the rocks near Great Falls; another at the wharf at Sixth Street. At Long Bridge, Georgetown, and as far as opposite Fort Washington, bodies, some without wounds, obviously drowned, continued to appear.

When the full extent of the debacle was evident (although the casualties would soon seem minuscule when compared to later battles), people began to point fingers. The most obvious person to blame for the defeat was Col. Edward Baker, who was in command, making tactical arrangements (which would have included plans for withdrawal, if needed) on the battlefield. But this did not sit well with his fellow congressmen, many of whom thought that their volunteer army should be commanded by volunteers—perhaps congressmen—not West Pointers.

The Joint Committee on the Conduct of the War was formed to get to the bottom of the Ball's Bluff catastrophe. According to one historian it became "the most influential, meddlesome, mischievous and baneful committee in the legislative history of the United States."

From the beginning it was clear they were looking for a scapegoat, not necessarily the truth about what happened at Ball's Bluff. That scapegoat was Brig. Gen. Charles Stone, who, after his testimony, was arrested in the middle of the night and sent to prison, disallowed visitors, never charged with a crime, and never told of what he was accused. Even his letters to the president, whom he had once guarded so faithfully, went unanswered. After 189 days, he was released, still without having had a trial. He would spend much of the rest of the war fighting the bureaucrats in Washington, the Joint Committee on the Conduct of the War, and continued attempts to besmirch his reputation. For the remainder of the conflict he was never given battlefield command of troops or a promotion. No doubt reading the handwriting on the wall, he resigned his commission before the end of the war.

Stone's curse continued: He fell into debt working for a coal mining company in Virginia. He enlisted, like a number of former Civil War officer outcasts (like Confederate officers), in the Egyptian army, where he remained until he returned to the United States in 1883. He died in 1887, no doubt still feeling cursed by a single small battle he thought he had under control.

Today, the smallest national cemetery in the nation sits atop Ball's Bluff, and holds the mostly unidentified dead from a battle that should never have been fought.

7

FREDERICKSBURG: CURSED BY LOCATION

In the annals of American history, some places stand out as a synonym for bloodshed—Bunker Hill, Gettysburg, the Little Bighorn. But they pale in comparison to one area in Virginia. Spotsylvania County and the city of Fredericksburg have the dubious distinction of being the most blood-soaked land in all of America because of four battles fought there during the Civil War, in which, as one publication put it, "100,000 fell."

Fredericksburg, by cruel accident of location, became cursed as a focal point for more than four years during the Civil War in Virginia. Situated equidistant from Washington, capital of the United States, and Richmond, capital of the Confederacy, it was directly on the route of the Union armies, with their "On to Richmond" strategy, and vital to the defense of the Confederate capital.

The city became a battleground twice during the war, and was the only American town to be shelled and pillaged into near rubble by an American army. Being the largest city in the area, it filled four times with the wounded and dying of four major Civil War battles fought in the vicinity. It was also the site of the first successful amphibious landing under fire by the US Army.

Beginning in November of 1862, Fredericksburg was occupied first by Confederates in the Army of Northern Virginia, commanded by Gen. Robert E. Lee. Later, in the spring of 1863, it would be captured by Federal forces.

But prior to that it was a thriving city with a history that reached back to before colonial times. Native Americans occupied the land that was first viewed by Capt. John Smith and his crew during their 1608 exploration of navigable waterways along the east coast of the New World. They got as far as "the Falls"—massive rock obstructions and low water—on the Rappahannock River, just beyond where the city would be established, before they turned back. No doubt they caught glimpses of the Manahoac Tribe, who already had established a settlement along the river.

By 1671 a land patent was granted for fifty acres, where Fredericksburg would later be sited, and forty settlers established homes and farms there. In 1727 the settlement became official, with a charter from the House of Burgesses in the capital of Williamsburg. The settlers named their town for Frederick, Prince of Wales.

Expansion was originally to the west. Governor Spotswood sponsored a settlement on the Rapidan River named Germanna in 1714. The cash crop was tobacco. In 1724, some 2,500,000 plants were being tended; the number doubled in two years, the demand for the burning leaf in England was so great. In 1730 a law was passed in Williamsburg requiring public inspection stations for tobacco, and that Spotsylvania's receiving and inspecting station would be in Fredericksburg. "Rolling roads," along which the barrel-shaped, thousand-pound hogsheads of dried tobacco were transported, were being built toward Fredericksburg. Later, in the early nineteenth century, "plank" roads and "turn-pikes" were constructed, leading across Spotsylvania to Fredericksburg's "port" on the Rappahannock River, which emptied into the Chesapeake Bay. Farmers and craftsmen from the counties to the west could transport their goods to a port connected to the world's oceans. Ferries were established to link Stafford County, just across the river, with Fredericksburg.

In 1738 young George Washington lived at Ferry Farm in Stafford, and necessarily spent a good deal of time in Fredericksburg. His brother built the Rising Sun Tavern there, and his sister married an up-and-coming businessman, Fielding Lewis. Eventually, Washington would buy a house for his mother in Fredericksburg, in which she would live out the remainder of her life. Other Colonial and Revolutionary War Era figures settled in the city: Revolutionary War generals Hugh Mercer and George Weedon; naval hero John Paul Jones, who spent time in Fredericksburg with his brother, whose house still stands; future president James Monroe, who had his law office in Fredericksburg; and Thomas Jefferson, who wrote the Virginia Statute for Religious Freedom in Fredericksburg.

By 1837, a north-south rail line, the Richmond, Fredericksburg and Potomac Railroad, would link Fredericksburg with the capital of Virginia and other parts of the South.

But ever since a few years after Capt. John Smith had first spied the Falls of the Rappahannock, the country had borne the burden of that "peculiar institution," slavery. No place would suffer as much for that curse as Fredericksburg and the adjacent Virginia counties, between 1862 and 1864.

In spite of the fact that before the Civil War Fredericksburg was a slave-trading location (the stone "slave auction block" still sits on a street corner), it was also on the route of the Underground Railroad. Its proximity to a river that emptied into the Chesapeake Bay, and boats to freedom guaranteed that.

Later, a national cemetery would be established high atop a major battlefield landmark, Marye's Heights, although it does not hold all the dead. The nature of "graves registration"—or lack thereof—in the Civil War would leave many dead unaccounted for. First, there were no "dog tags" (government-supplied personal identification tags) for the soldiers. Personal correspondence found on the bodies was used to identify them. If someone had already gone through their pockets and the paper had blown away, well, that was one more brave soldier who ended up in the "Unknown" section of the national cemetery, with his family at home wondering why his letters suddenly stopped coming.

Bodies were buried first where they fell on the battlefield. If their comrades did it, they may have supplied a wooden headboard with a penciled inscription. If that got knocked over or separated from the grave, the rains would soon erase the gravesite.

And if the forgotten and misplaced dead have anything to do with perpetuating a curse, Fredericksburg historians have tallied more than one hundred thousand dead in its long history. The only problem: There are only five thousand marked graves.

8

FIELDING LEWIS:
CURSED FOR HIS
PATRIOTISM

One of the more prominent citizens of Colonial Fredericksburg was Fielding Lewis. Having learned the retail business from his father at the Lewis Store in Fredericksburg, he became a successful, wealthy businessman. He also married well. His second marriage was to George Washington's sister Betty. With Betty he had eleven children and built "Kenmore Mansion" on their plantation land (now incorporated into the City of Fredericksburg). Mary Ball Washington, Betty and George's mother, visited frequently from Ferry Farm, across the Rappahannock River, and later, from her home a few blocks away in Fredericksburg, purchased for her by George.

Lewis was active in the political scene of early Virginia as a justice of the county court, entailing a good bit of travel from his home. He also began buying up land starting in 1750, by the thousands of acres. As well, he and a partner had business interests to the west in Winchester, Virginia. Upon the death of his father in 1754, Fielding inherited more land, and full control of the Lewis business transactions in Virginia. He divided his land holdings in Fredericksburg and began selling off the lots. He speculated with his brother-in-law George on an unsuccessful venture to drain the Dismal Swamp for land.

Starting in 1765, he spurred the county into establishing a school for the children of slaves, against the wishes of slaveholders, who argued that they needed the labor during planting and harvesting seasons. The school only lasted five years, closing in 1770.

Beginning around 1764, Lewis got into the shipping business, eventually owning a small fleet of transport ships, capable of both navigating the rivers of Virginia and cruising the oceans.

He and his brother-in-law, George—after his career in surveying, and as a soldier in the French and Indian War—became burgesses, and often traveled to the capital of Williamsburg together during the 1770s.

But revolution was in the air in America. By 1775 a "Continental Congress" had been meeting. In May they appointed George Washington to command a continental army. Virginia was to raise two regiments, and in August forwarded plans to establish a gun factory in Fredericksburg, naming Fielding Lewis as one of the commissioners to oversee it. His workload apparently became overburdening since, for the first time in thirty years, he ceased making his faithful entries in the family Bible.

His marital connections, at first, seemed a godsend, when thousands of pounds of money were promised for the "gunn manufactory." He wrote to his brother-in-law that he expected to be producing twelve guns per day. In addition to his political duties, he also tendered his services to the church.

He was in the process of building a mansion house on 1,200 acres on the outskirts of Fredericksburg; named "Kenmore," the house did not come into full use until 1819, long after Lewis's death. The building was classic in design and elaborate on the interior, with some of the finest interior stucco plastering ever seen in this country, provided by an indentured servant shared by George Washington.

By the spring of 1777, Fielding Lewis's gunnery employed some sixty persons and was turning out about twenty muskets (with bayonets) per week.

The war, however, was going badly for the Americans. Defeat after defeat, and hardships such as the winters at Valley Forge and Jockey Hollow, near Morristown, New Jersey, tested the nascent American character. Washington won some victories, but perhaps realized that, rather than defeating the world's most powerful army in battle, he simply must hold out longer. The British, it turned out, with interests around the globe, would soon tire of the pesky rebels on the American continent.

The long duration and expense of the war, however, was catastrophic for the continental economy. Depreciation of paper money and the increased printing of it led to the eventual worthlessness of the paper. Inflation hit everyone hard, but certainly some of the hardest hit were entrepreneurs with heavy investments in the future. Fielding Lewis, who owned the largest commercial enterprise in Fredericksburg, certainly felt the impact keenly.

By the end of 1779, the government had advanced fifteen thousand pounds to the gun manufactory, but because of inflation, Lewis needed to put in another 4,100 pounds of his own money, expecting to be repaid someday by the government.

More and more money was printed and loan certificates were issued, promising a 6 percent return in three years. The ever trusting and patriotic Fielding Lewis invested 19,000 pounds in the certificates. Since paper money was so devalued, the Virginia Assembly began an enforced collection of commodities as taxes. During this time period, Fielding Lewis's health began to deteriorate. Nevertheless, all the while he kept arms from the manufactory flowing. Lewis poured more of his own money into the company to keep it running. The workers at the gun factory petitioned the colonial government for a raise in pay, to just over 7 pounds per day. The government felt their request was "reasonable," and so granted them the raise, but never granted Lewis the money, placing an additional financial burden on Fielding Lewis. To keep the factory supplying arms to the army of his country, he did the only thing he could do: He began to sell his own property.

After selling various tracts of his land, Lewis came up with enough cash to keep the gunnery running through 1780. At the end of the year, Lewis and his partner were paid by the government—in tobacco.

Congress never got around to repaying him fully for his own investment in his country's independence, and Fielding Lewis died in 1781, just after the British surrender at Yorktown, still believing that

Congress would pay him for the arms he had supplied that helped to win the war. But the newly established government never did, and his indebtedness for patriotically supporting the cause of independence passed down to his heirs.

So Fielding Lewis, if not cursed for his love of country and fidelity to the cause of independence, certainly was treated poorly for it. And he seems to have left an imprint in the mansion.

Workers and guides at Kenmore (currently being restored to its eighteenth-century splendor) have seen a misty figure in colonial garb standing in the study, poring over ledger books, apparently concerned with mounting bills, pondering where the next dollar is going to come from to pay his gunsmiths. They have also seen smoke coming from the chimney of one of the outbuildings, once used by Lewis as an office. When they inspected it, they found no fire burning. Could it be Fielding Lewis, still toiling to catch up on his Bible entries?

9

THE RISING
SUN TAVERN

Near the corner of Fauquier and Caroline Streets in Fredericksburg is the Rising Sun Tavern, which has a long history, and stands as another monument to one of Fredericksburg's most famous sons, George Washington. It was built by Washington's younger brother, and its original floorboards have felt the footfall of famous early Americans, including James Madison, John Paul Jones, Thomas Jefferson, George Mason, John Marshall, and, of course, Washington himself.

In 1792, John Frazer became the first tavern keeper in the Rising Sun Tavern. When he died in an upstairs room, his wife, Elizabeth Fox Frazer, became the second tavern keeper there. Throughout the years, employees have told of hearing heavy boots walking in rooms known to be unoccupied. Recently, a relative of John Frazer visited the tavern and reported that, according to the family, his ancestor was indeed a large, heavy man.

Within just the past few years an employee was standing in the tavern room looking out the door at a strategically placed mirror, by which employees can watch what goes on down the entire hall behind them. Standing in the tavern room, she heard the unmistakable sound of heavy boots coming down the hall. She looked into the mirror to see who it was, but, in spite of the continued heavy footfalls, she could see no one in the hallway reflected in the mirror. Also in the tavern room, a number of visitors and employees have reported seeing what they call a "floating glow." It remains for several seconds, then vanishes.

More often than should be expected, photographs taken inside the house do not come out. Special permission from the owner is needed to take pictures inside the Rising Sun, and so most photos taken inside are of a special nature—professionals working for magazines and the like. There was a professional photographer who had been taking pictures with his expensive thirty-five-millimeter camera all around town. He came to the Rising Sun and took numerous pictures of a scene upstairs, using a stool as a prop. He returned a year later and explained to the staff that all of his photos of Fredericksburg had developed just fine, except for those he had taken in the "Tap Room." Not a single one of those came out. Later, a group of students from Virginia Commonwealth University visited for a class project, to videotape in the tavern. Their camera worked fine, except for the sound, which, try as they might, they could not get to work.

An employee was standing in the doorway when a second employee approached the door and asked, "Did you bring your friend to work with you today?" When the answer was "no," the inquiring employee turned suddenly and went around the back to enter the house. When asked later why she had gone around the back to enter, she said she had positively seen a woman standing behind the first employee when she inquired about her friend, and suddenly realized that the person she saw, who was not her fellow employee's friend, was not even of this earth.

Upon closing the tavern, a heavy wooden bar is always placed across the doorway to the cellar. As she was about to bar the door, an employee was called away by the only other employee still in the building, so she wedged the bar against the corner of the door. She returned a minute later to see the heavy bar lying on the floor at least two lengths away from where she had left it—too far away for it to have fallen—and perfectly parallel with the edge of the rug, as if it had been carefully placed there.

Two women employees were alone in the Tap Room, sitting on the stools. Although they were alone in the building, they heard heavy footsteps stomp diagonally across the floor in the room directly above their heads. One of them summoned up enough courage to climb the stairs and investigate. No one was in the room above their heads. She went back down and resumed her seat next to her fellow employee, explaining what she had—or actually, had not—seen. Ten minutes later, the heavy footfalls were heard again, this time re-crossing the room in the opposite direction, just a few feet above their heads. The mystery, apparently, had lost its novelty; neither volunteered to inspect the room again.

And there was the story of the young woman who was dressed in the colonial garb the employees wear in the Rising Sun Tavern. Several other employees were standing at the bottom of the stairs as she started up to the second floor. Suddenly she was stopped from ascending the stairs; all the employees present saw her full skirt pull straight out as if by some invisible hand grabbing on to it. Moments later, it was released, and someone in the group, attempting to explain the bizarre experience, commented, "John Frazer did it."

As an adjunct to this author's "Ghosts of Fredericksburg Tours," we had offered several "Paranormal Investigation Weekends," during which our guests were allowed to investigate a few famous haunted buildings in the city, one of which was the Rising Sun Tavern.

On March 17, 2012, our investigation of the Tavern was a one-of-a-kind event . . . in more ways than one.

Our method for paranormal investigations is different from the investigations one sees on television. Where they use their equipment to allegedly locate ghosts in an environment, we teach an "intuition-forward" method of finding paranormal anomalies. We instruct and encourage our participants to hone their own sensitivity to the environment. We then ask them to follow their own feelings as to where they want to go to investigate. More often than not, the novice investigators leave with a newfound confidence in their own ability to perform a paranormal investigation.

The following is the verbatim report I wrote up after this investigation of the Rising Sun Tavern. It includes one of the most bizarre and unexplainable events, seemingly involving a curse, that I've ever been involved in.

RISING SUN TAVERN INVESTIGATION

March 17, 2012, 5:15–6:45 p.m.

I was assigned to supervise the investigations in the cellar of the Tavern. Joni and Vicky were the first two investigators. After a preliminary moment or two acclimating and focusing near the stairs, I asked them to determine, by intuition, where in the cellar they were drawn. They both pointed to the far corner from the stairs.

We walked over and saw that there was another set of stairs leading to a door that apparently led outside. (Remember, this was my first time in the cellar, too.) It was determined that Joni would be the first medium and Vicky would be the first scribe. Joni received the name "John," which she later determined to be "Jonathan"—perhaps the "Jonathan" Laine (the medium we were working with that night) had talked with on our preliminary investigation)—and was using her pendulum. The session hadn't gone more than a minute or two when we heard a strange "whooshing," a wind-like sound that sounded canned, like something out of a B-movie. Immediately after that there was male laughter—not sinister, but, once again sounding "canned." At first I thought it was coming from my recorder, then from the door, then from the air ducts. The whole thing lasted three or four seconds. I thought about pulling out my recorder, but thought, because the sound was so canned and realistic, that it was probably someone from the Tavern playing a prank, a recording through the ductwork. Joni and Vicky looked at me. I shook my head and said that it must be somebody playing a joke on us. We continued the investigation.

Vicky's experience with the pendulum was remarkable. She had never used a pendulum before, and had chosen what we think was a green jasper. After about five minutes of questioning Jonathan, she said she could see her pendulum glowing. I looked at it and saw a vertical streak of light on the side toward her. I moved around, as did Joni, to try and find a light source that was hitting it to make it glow. It wasn't the sun coming in through the basement window nearby; the sun was hitting another part of the cellar floor and not the pendulum. I even blocked out the incandescent light hitting the ductwork, but the glow continued. As I watched, there was a small (one-eighth-inch) ball of light glowing in the pendulum crystal on the side away from Vicki that grew to about one-quarter inch, faded back to one-eighth inch, grew back to one-quarter inch, then faded back to one-eighth inch.

(I have seen things appear in pendulums once before, at Little Round Top Farm [in Gettysburg, Pennsylvania] investigation. Investigators said they saw faces in the quartz crystal, but I could only see a glow.)

Regarding the noise in the basement: I'm wondering if the wind noise was in some way a carrier wave for the laughter, or something preparing the environment for the communication. More interestingly, just an hour or so later, the whole group heard something similar back at the Marriott conference room.

We had set up the psychometry experiment at the table in the front of the room on the round table. One of the items was an old box belonging to D_____ and J_____. One time, when it was opened, there was a noise—low white noise, perhaps the wind sound again, coming from the back corner of the room. D_____ accused J_____ of making it, but he stood and opened the door to see if anyone was out in the hall. Within a few seconds, we all heard laughter coming from the corner of the room behind me. I stood and went out into the hall and saw no one except J_____, who had again gone out into the hall to see if there was anyone out there. The nearest person to the room was a guy at the bar with a cell phone. I had thought upon reflection that the sound may have been a ringtone; it sort of had that tinny, canned quality. But the phone of the guy at the bar rang while I was out there and that wasn't the ringtone. I still cannot rule out a random ringtone of someone exiting the restroom, which was about twenty feet from the conference-room door, or someone at the bar. A ringtone consisting of exactly the same kind of laughter we had heard at the Rising Sun?

One thing I forgot to add: Thinking that someone was playing a prank on us while we were in the cellar, I told Joni and Vicky not to worry, that I would catch the prankster when the next group came into the cellar and the same noise was played. The next group came, and I waited for the "recording" to play. Nothing. Surely, I thought, the next group will tempt the prankster into playing the whooshing sound and B-movie canned laughter. But the next group's experience did not draw out the sounds.

Finally, when the investigation was over and I climbed the stairs to the first floor, I walked to the manager of the Tavern.

"Very funny," I said.

She gave me a quizzical look. "What are you talking about?"

I had a smirk on my face. "You know; playing a recording of wind sound and laughter into the cellar."

She looked at me like I was crazy, which I was starting to feel.

I continued: "You mean, you didn't play a recording through the ducts or speakers into the cellar about a half-hour ago?" I had seen some small speakers attached to the rafters, although that was not where I had heard the sound coming from.

"No. Why would I do that? Besides, we haven't used those speakers in years."

I remembered the stairs and the defunct door to the outside.

"Was anyone outside the building, anyone who could have made a noise?"

"Nobody even knows you're here doing an investigation. We kept it secret."

To add to the mystery, the old box which seemed to trigger the noises to repeat themselves in the brand-new Marriott belonged to D_____ and J_____. I found out that at the time Joni, Vicky, and I were investigating that one area of the cellar, D_____ and J_____ were investigating the room directly above us.

The question lingers in my mind: Was it something in the antique box that triggered the noises in the modern Marriott? And the other question one must ask is, was it something D_____ and J_____ brought with them on the trip to Fredericksburg?

10

THE CURSE OF
SLAVERY AND
"THE CHIMNEYS"

Fredericksburg was named after Frederick, the Prince of Wales at the time. It only made sense to the early inhabitants, loyal British subjects that they were, to name the streets after the rest of his family.

"The Chimneys," located on the corner of Caroline and Charlotte Streets, was built around 1770 by an immigrant Scottish merchant named John Glassell. Loyal to the Crown, when the Revolution broke out, he left his property to his brother and returned to Scotland. The property changed hands many times over the centuries and has assumed numerous incarnations since then, from private residence to numerous eating establishments. Over the years it has been the source of dozens of unexplainable, ghostly tales.

Apparently, one of the early occupants, a young woman, played the harp in the parlor, for it is from this area that the sweet strains of a phantom harp are heard upon occasion, playing a melody many decades off the list of popular songs. Sometimes the refrain is accompanied by a ghostly singer, as invisible as the harp and harpist.

Years after the harp and its player were gone from The Chimneys, some occupants of the house bought a piano. One evening a young woman sat down and began to accompany herself. Partway into the song, she heard the front door (which, at that time, was the one facing the Rappahannock River) open and close. She was surprised to hear footsteps approach. She knew there were guests out front and called out a request for the person trying to frighten her to identify himself. The only answer was the plodding, phantom footsteps which, by now, had reached the doorway to the room in which she was playing. She turned apprehensively toward the sound, but as the footfalls approached the piano, she could see no one. Her piano recital came to an abrupt end when someone, quite invisible, sat down on the piano bench next to her and placed an unseen but icy hand upon her shoulder.

One particular night in the early twentieth century, when The Chimneys was still a residence, a woman was awakened by a chill in the air. The chill grew perceptibly colder as she approached her youngest son's bedroom. She took a blanket from a closet and entered his room. To her astonishment, there was another male child apparently asleep in the bed next to her son. She could not identify him because his face was half covered with the sheet, but she assumed that perhaps her sleeping husband had invited one of the neighbor boys to spend the night. She covered the two, and went back to bed herself. The next morning when her husband awakened, she asked him who the boy was he had invited to spend the night with their son. She was met with an incredulous look and the assertion that he had not invited anyone to spend the night. At that moment, her son came down for breakfast and confirmed that indeed, he had slept alone that night. And while the woman's original mission was to cover her son to ward off the cold, the temperature—at least in the rest of the house—had been overly warm.

Ghosts at The Chimneys are not a new phenomenon. Dr. Brodie Herndon, who owned the house in the mid-nineteenth century, claimed that the house was haunted. Some of the paranormal events he recorded continue to this day, such as doorknobs being turned by invisible hands and doors opening by themselves. Apparently in Mr. Brodie's time a woman saw her uncle standing in one of the rooms across the hall from her. By the time she entered the room, it was empty. This apparition is what is known as a "harbinger," for her uncle died three days later.

And auditory apparitions, the most common of all paranormal events, also occur; for example, the sound of china crashing to the floor. Upon inspection of the room and floor, nothing is found to be amiss. Heavy footsteps are heard in the hall when no one is there; doors are heard slamming, and occasionally, someone will watch as a rocking chair starts moving back and forth—with no one seated in it.

Some of the more recent happenings involve child ghosts. The apparition of a little boy is seen roaming about upstairs. There is the rumor of a little boy who fell from the balcony to his death many years ago. He also apparently doesn't like a certain door upstairs to be closed, because, as often as those who have rented The Chimneys for business close it and leave at night, the next morning when they reopen, they find that the door is open. Witnesses have reported seeing the apparition of a grown woman, as well as one of a little girl who walks the floor upstairs, and then is seen to vanish.

Old tales are one thing; they can be written off as hearsay, with a kernel of truth that, with retelling, has bloomed into a fully formed horror story. But it was an experience that occurred during a paranormal investigation in 2006 that convinced this author that there just may be something to the continued haunting of the old structure with the prominent chimneys in Fredericksburg.

Stories about the famous Underground Railroad, that clandestine matrix of people, routes, and safe houses for runaway slaves in antebellum America, are as mysterious as they are romantic. Most of what we know about the system of transferring slaves from slaveholding states to freedom comes from *after* the Civil War, since harboring escaped slaves, throughout most of American history, was a crime, and those involved were reluctant to speak about it. In spite of that, the Virginia Abolition Society was formed in the 1780s.

But legislators representing slaveholders fought back. In the Fugitive Slave Act of 1793, rights to slaves as property became constitutional. Because of the Fugitive Slave Act of 1850, it became a violation of federal law to assist escaping slaves, who were forcibly returned to their masters, and heavy fines and jail terms were inflicted upon those aiding slaves' escape. Regardless, by 1830 the Underground Railroad was in full operation in both the North and the South.

Railroad terminology was used to throw off slave catchers: Safe houses were *depots* or *stations* located one night's walk apart; *conductors* were guides to escaping slaves; *agents* offered their homes as day shelters for escapees; *superintendents* controlled the operations in an entire state. During the day, slaves were hidden in barns, beneath floorboards, in false rooms, the cog-pits of mills, and damp cellars. They often waited days for forged "documents of passage" to arrive. Night escapes were on foot, or in false bottoms in wagons, on the top of railroad cars, by canoe, schooner, or steamer. The Chesapeake Bay was sought because of its access into the North, so the waterways draining into the Bay—such as the Rappahannock—were desired routes. Indeed, several maps of the routes of the escapees on the Underground Railroad show Fredericksburg in the center.

Like so many places on the Underground Railroad, there is no documented evidence that The Chimneys was ever used as a depot on the famous escape route. There is, however, spectral evidence from the Other World that someone, desperate to escape, remained in the cellar of the building far too long. This is a story of two kinds of escape: one from slavery, the other from death.

THE CHIMNEYS INVESTIGATION
April 21, 2006

On the evening of April 21, 2006, Julie, one of the spirit liaisons (or mediums) used by our team during paranormal investigations, explored The Chimneys, along with several others interested in the paranormal history of the building. After getting her impressions of several of the rooms, including the strong presence of a seafarer, she descended into the cellar. Julie approached the main area of the cellar and suddenly commented, "I feel like I can't leave, but I'm not a prisoner and I'm not locked in."

"Channeling" is a psychic phenomenon wherein the medium becomes a conduit for the deceased, feeling, moving, and speaking as if they were the dead person, sometimes even using his or her voice. Julie was later asked if she was channeling someone dead from the past and she answered no, that she was merely repeating, verbatim, what she was hearing in the cellar that night. According to Carol Nesbitt, the author's wife who accompanied her into the cellar, after passing through the door into the room, Julie received the name "Nicodemus."

Julie's commentary, which appears below, indicated a spirit with limited verbal skills, "waiting for papers."

"Can't leave without papers. Miss Hattie bring papers. Can't read, can't write, don't know what in papers. Need papers to leave.

"Others come, get papers, leave. Don't understand . . .

"People in house don't know I here."

[Carol asks Julie if his name is Nicodemus.]

"No, just what they call me. Hattie not her name, just what they call her."

Carol called me into the cellar and Julie asked me to attempt to get some EVP—electronic voice phenomena. EVP is the recording of voices, apparently of the deceased, using electronic means. It began with the advent of magnetic tape (although some claim that Thomas Edison received unheard voices on his wax roll recorder), and continues to the present, with researchers today utilizing digital recorders. My technique is to ask a question out loud that is pertinent to the past, saying it into a digital recorder, then pause, with the recorder set on "voice activation." In the cellar of The Chimneys, in complete silence, the machine began to record.

Two sessions were attempted. The first session yielded rough, growling, staccato answers to my questions. Prior to the second session, Julie recommended that I tell "Nicodemus" that he could go now, that he didn't need his papers, and that he didn't need to wait for Hattie, which I did.

As I stood there in the darkened cellar, I felt an extremely cold spot touch my right arm and remain there for about five seconds. Then it was replaced by a hot sensation, then back to regular temperature. After the session, I mentioned this to Julie, who was standing to my right. She, too, had felt the presence of "Nicodemus" as he passed between us and left the cellar—free, as the old slave song says, "free at last."

11

CURSED ON CAROLINE STREET, AND THE WHITE LADY OF CHATHAM

One of the great curses visited upon America before the Civil War was the forced enslavement of fellow human beings. Many Southerners emancipated their slaves long before the war; others, with large farms to manage, realized that they just couldn't get along without slavery.

Fredericksburg was part of the slaveholding South. Of the 3,000 inhabitants of Fredericksburg in 1835, 1,124 were slaves. African Americans were allegedly bought and sold on the corner of William and Charles Streets on the auction block, which was used, among other things, for the display and sale of human beings. It is interesting to imagine that along with the ghosts of tens of thousands of Civil War soldiers—who died to either free slaves, or to maintain a lifestyle that encompassed slavery—there could also be the spirits of long-dead slaves, still in bonds, of a more ethereal, but still unbreakable, kind.

People think that ghost stories are relegated to the past. This is not true.

This one comes to us from the last week in July of 2005. An employee in a cafe on Caroline Street was looking for something. They entered an upstairs room that had been habitually sealed off since it had last been cleaned. Indeed, the person found something, but it was not what she expected. Imprinted across the floor were the footprints of a large male. They were bare footprints, etched in white, walking from one side of the abandoned room to the other, and back again, as if pacing, and waiting for something to happen, or someone to come and release them from this centuries-long incarceration.

Someone in authority was called and shown the footprints. "Well, let's wash them off," was the order from the boss. But try as they might, the footprints would not wash off. They were apparently made of something indelible. The room was closed, but inspected frequently after that. Slowly, over a couple of weeks, the footprints faded from sight, returning to the unseen world from whence they had come.

From the corner of William and Caroline, one can see the bridge that spans the Rappahannock River. Across the river on the bluff sits Chatham, built between 1768 and 1771 by William Fitzhugh. George Washington spent many happy hours there. It purports to be the only house in America visited by both Washington and Abraham Lincoln. According to historians, young Robert E. Lee courted his wife to be, Miss Mary Custis, in Chatham's lovely rose garden. During the Battle of Fredericksburg in December of 1862, it was known as the Lacy House, after its owner, and was used as a headquarters for the Union Army. It was also used as a hospital during the Battle of Fredericksburg, where both Clara Barton, founder of the Red Cross, and American poet Walt Whitman nursed wounded soldiers. It is now owned by the National Park Service, and serves as headquarters for the Fredericksburg and Spotsylvania National Military Park.

There are periodic sightings, like clockwork, of the famous White Lady of Chatham. The wife of a former owner in the early twentieth century saw her on several occasions in the famous garden of Chatham, strolling casually along the path leading to the terrace below, then vanishing as suddenly as she had appeared. Her story is as mysterious as it is sad.

The story comes down to us through Marguerite DuPont Lee in her 1930s book, *Virginia Ghosts*. She tells of Mrs. Randolph Howard, who confided to only a few friends that she had seen a strange woman in white, pacing up and down the garden path which led by marble steps to the terrace below. It was sometime in the afternoon, June 21. (Many people believe that ghosts only appear at night, but this author's personal research of over 1,200 accounts confirms that at least 45 percent of sightings occur during the day.) She had kept the sighting a secret; she didn't want to frighten her servants. Sometime later she was entertaining a friend who happened to be a scholar of French literature. He began to tell her of an interesting discovery he had made while poring over some books written in French in a library in Newark, New Jersey. He was leafing through a collection of ghost stories when the names "Washington" and "Chatham" leapt from the pages. He began to tell Mrs. Howard the story.

It appears that a young Englishwoman of a well-to-do family fell in love with a common "dry-salter," or taxidermist. The union was frowned upon by the girl's father, so they made plans for an elopement. They were soon discovered by her father. He immediately took his daughter to America where they met the Fitzhughs and stayed for a while at Chatham. The ardent dry-salter followed, clandestinely contacted the young lady, and they planned their elopement once again. Again the father discovered the plan and locked her in her room at Chatham every night.

But the dry-salter was persistent. He planned her escape via a rope ladder from her room in Chatham to his boat moored on the river below. At the appointed hour, she descended the ladder and dropped into the arms of none other than Gen. George Washington himself, a friend of the owners of Chatham. The plot had been discovered by an aide to the general, who had the dry-salter locked up. Washington took the girl to her father who, exasperated, returned with her back to England. There he married her off quickly. In spite of bearing her husband ten children, she apparently continued to dream of her first love and their planned elopement from Chatham. On June 21, 1790, on her deathbed, she predicted that she would return to Chatham from the Other World to walk the terrace, her favorite spot, as a spirit.

She apparently does return. It was she whom Mrs. Howard saw that afternoon, strolling through the terrace garden. She returns punctually, every seven years, on June 21, the anniversary of her death, and walks sometime between noon and midnight. The next anniversary of her appearance will be in 2021.

Chatham, during the Civil War, became a Union headquarters and hospital for some thirteen months. The owner at the time was James Horace Lacy, who had joined the Confederate Army and become a staff officer. When the Northerners took over his home, his wife was forced out. The months that the Federals occupied it were not kind to the house.

In addition to becoming a hub for the Union Army, it also became a hospital during the December, 1862, battle and the second Battle of Fredericksburg, associated with the Chancellorsville Campaign in the spring of 1863. The former fighting saw some 130 Union soldiers buried on the grounds of Chatham. The poet Walt Whitman described the scene: Outside of the operating room near a tree (which may be the one still standing there) he saw "a heap of amputated feet, legs, arms, hands, etc.—about a load for a one-horse cart. Several dead bodies lie near, each covered with its brown woolen blanket." Later, most of those buried at Chatham were removed to the national cemetery on Marye's Heights in Fredericksburg. During the second battle in Fredericksburg, nearly one thousand wounded Union soldiers were brought to Chatham for care.

When the Lacys returned after the war, the destruction to the house and environs was devastating: Human bloodstains had ruined the floors, soldiers' graffiti had wrecked the walls, and the fields and yards had been churned up by marching soldiers, wagons, and artillery horses. Try as they might, they couldn't restore it, so they sold Chatham in 1872.

The owners attempted, over the years, to bring the place back to its antebellum glory, but to no avail. Finally, industrialist John Lee Pratt purchased it in 1931, preserved and restored the manor, and left it in his will to the National Park Service in 1975.

What happened to the Civil War owners, the Lacys? It appears that they, like the McLean family of Manassas, were cursed by the Civil War to never escape its far-reaching tentacles. They moved to their "summer" house, Mrs. Lacy's family home, "Ellwood"—built, of all places, where the Battle of the Wilderness was soon to be fought.

12

FREDERICKSBURG REOCCUPIED BY THE ENEMY

From its colonial heritage to the horror of being the focal point of four major Civil War battles, Fredericksburg has seen more history and more human tragedy than virtually any other city in America. Between 1862 and 1864, more than one hundred thousand men and boys became casualties in the fighting in and around the town; most were brought to Fredericksburg to be operated upon, recover, or perish.

On December 11, 1862, after midnight, engineers from the Union Army began construction of pontoon bridges at two sites across the Rappahannock River from Fredericksburg, and another farther downstream. They had gotten the bridges partway across when infantrymen from Mississippi stationed at the river heard the suspicious—but anticipated—noises of construction on the river. Gen. William Barksdale's Mississippians held the waterfront along Sophia Street and back to Princess Anne, utilizing fortifications they had dug and buildings in the city.

On the bridges the engineers, mostly hidden in the early-morning fog, heard the bells of St. George's Episcopal Church toll the 5:00 a.m. hour. Ten minutes later, with the bridges built halfway across the river, they heard an officer from the Fredericksburg side of the river shout "Fire!" Sheets of flame flashed in the fog and Union soldiers tumbled, dead and dying, onto the bridges and into the icy water. Those who survived ran for their lives back to the shore.

Union artillery batteries stationed on the opposite shore above Fredericksburg opened fire on the city. Depending upon which account you read—private soldiers' or officers'—the shelling was either devastating or worthless. One private said he saw wooden boards and bricks fly; another, that every shot struck and broke down walls and chimneys; a staff officer thought the damage was out of proportion to the amount of shells sent into the town; another thought the bombardment was inefficient.

The bombardment did not accomplish driving Barksdale's men out of their nests, and they continued to hold up the crossing. By 12:30 p.m., Union Army commander Ambrose Burnside ordered another bombardment on the city. Again chimneys and brick walls fell, some onto Confederates ensconced in cellars, or on Southern officers trying to command. Union artillerists realized, however, when they fired at clapboard houses, that the shells passed right through, only aiding Confederate sharpshooters by providing more firing ports. By 2:30 p.m., Burnside realized his entire battle plans were in jeopardy unless he solved the problem presented by a handful of Rebels with rifles.

The engineers first came up with a plan and passed it on to an artillery officer, who gave it to Burnside. He asked for volunteers to man the pontoon boats and row across the river to drive the Confederate riflemen back and establish a foothold on the waterfront at Fredericksburg.

Rowing literally like their lives depended upon it, volunteers from the 7th Michigan got about two-thirds of the way across and realized that the enemy's fire had slackened; they had gained cover from the bank of the river. The house-to-house fighting was savage. Some of the Michigan men used the bayonet freely on Confederates, whether they surrendered or not. After about twenty minutes, the Rebels were driven from the riverbank streets, and more Union troops arrived. The Michigan troops had pioneered a new tactic that would be a mainstay of the wars in the next century: They accomplished the first successful amphibious landing under fire in United States military history.

After initially fighting the delaying action through the streets of Fredericksburg, the Confederates withdrew to the heights west of the city, there to repulse numerous, bloody Union attacks two days later.

Union troops occupied the town, prying into private pantries, pilfering what they needed, and peering out windows of private homes, looking for the enemy, or even their own provost guard.

According to a woman whose family has lived in Fredericksburg for well over a century, renovation was going on in one of the historic buildings along Caroline Street near William. The new owner had spent all day tearing up old carpeting. He had finished for the day and rolled it up against the wall in the hall in order to facilitate the workmen removing it the next day. It is well known in paranormal circles that, whenever there is a renovation to a historic building, there is more likelihood of paranormal experiences occurring. It is almost as if the spirits do not want their routine, their status quo, disturbed. So it was in this case.

Trash men were coming the next afternoon. As he left for the night, the owner told the workmen to remove the rolled-up carpet first thing the next morning and put it by the curb. The next morning, when he arrived at the worksite, before the trash pickup, there was no carpet at the curb. At first he was angry, because he knew that their disobedience would cost him time. He sought out the foreman and gave him a dressing-down. The foreman then took him upstairs to show him why they hadn't removed the carpet. When his men had arrived to work that morning, the carpet was no longer in the hall. He opened the door to the room and showed the owner: The carpet was there, laid down again, tacks in place.

The owner was rightfully concerned, and apparently felt right away that there was something paranormal going on.

He called his priest.

The priest came to inspect the area. He walked upstairs to the room, cautiously opened the door, and was greeted by the sight of several ghostly Union soldiers peering out of the windows as their earthly forms would have done, over a century before. The priest left and told the owner that he'd pray for the souls to be on their way.

Upon leaving, he uttered something ominous, spawned, perhaps, by something else he had witnessed in that room, but would not talk about. He said he would also pray for the owner.

13

SMYTHE'S COTTAGE:
THE CURSE OF
CONSCIENCE

There is a small building on the corner of Princess Anne and Fauquier Streets in Fredericksburg that predates the Civil War. It, like
so many buildings in the historic city of Fredericksburg, has been preserved and has been given many roles by its owners over the years:
private residence, restaurant, teahouse.

Though ownership and the name has changed since, during the
early days of the twenty-first century, it was known as "Smythe's
Cottage," and served fine Virginia-based dishes as a restaurant for a
number of years.

According to the owners of Smythe's Cottage, patrons and
employees have experienced unexplainable phenomena over the
years. For example, prior to opening, an employee will walk through
the several rooms used for dining, lighting candles on the tables.
Passing back through the room she just visited, she will see that some
of the candles have been blown out. Setting tables with silverware
in Smythe's Cottage before opening is often frustrating: When the
server returns to the room that was just set, the silverware is moved
out of place. Both things occur when there are no other people in
the room. Those, and other seemingly paranormal phenomena, are
blamed on a woman the owners call "Elizabeth," who is believed to
have committed suicide by hanging herself in the stairway leading
to the second floor.

Elizabeth, according to legend, was either a stanch Union sympathizer, or sometime during the war, for some unexplained but whispered reason, became one. With her husband away fighting for the Confederacy and Fredericksburg occupied by Union soldiers during the Civil War, one can only speculate as to why she would pass important information on to the enemy, although it easily could have been done. It is also rumored that the building during the war was used as a bordello, no doubt by occupying Union troops. Whether Elizabeth was involved in this type of fraternization with the enemy is unknown, but the rumor is that, whatever she was doing, her husband caught her and accused her of treason toward the South, and infidelity to him. One night, apparently driven by guilt, she went to the top of the stairs and hanged herself.

The children of the owner (when the building was known as Smythe's Cottage) had experiences on the second floor of the house. One, when he was eleven years old, watched as the closet doors began to open by themselves while he was the only person in the room. Frightened, he left the room rapidly. His younger brother, at age nine, saw a whitish mist begin to slowly float from the same closet. More recently, a diner in the back room of the restaurant saw a short, heavyset woman wearing a long, dark, "old-fashioned" skirt and white apron, moving swiftly past his table as if on a mission, going out into the garden. Interestingly enough, some ghost hunters were conducting a paranormal investigation at the time. The investigators hurried to catch up with her, but by the time they reached the garden, which is surrounded by a high wooden fence, she had vanished.

Other paranormal events were recorded while the investigators were there. In the same room where Elizabeth had been seen, a bowl containing packets of sugar and artificial sweetener crashed to the floor and broke. No one had been in the room when it happened. The investigators caught some odd lights on videotape, moving in opposite directions—obviously not reflections from car lights, which would have been moving in the same direction, over and over, as cars passed on the one-way Princess Anne Street. And the closet door which the owner's son had seen beginning to open (before he beat a hasty retreat) was recorded on the tape as moving, ever so slightly, as if someone was trying, but failing, to open it.

While my wife Carol and I were developing a walking tour of Fredericksburg, highlighting the ghost stories of the town, we had lunch at Smythe's Cottage, and, of course, heard about all of the ghost stories chronicled here, as well as two more.

We were told that once, while walking past the stairs, at the top of which Elizabeth had allegedly committed suicide by hanging herself, an employee's eye was caught by a motion. As she looked up the stairs she saw an elongated mist about the length of a human body, swinging back and forth across the opening to the second floor.

Right next to the entrance to the stairway was a framed photograph of Union hero, Gen. Ulysses S. Grant, which the owners had hung with a sense of fairness to both sides who had struggled so fiercely around Fredericksburg. And while Grant did not command Union forces at Fredericksburg, his image in a Confederate town, in the home of a former Confederate soldier, was apparently too much even for one dead for decades. The picture was always crooked, having to be straightened constantly by the employees. Although the cottage was dozens of yards off the main street of Princess Anne, I asked if it might not be the rumble of traffic causing the picture to tilt.

The owner said, yes, that might be the reason. It might be the reason, too, for the picture to have fallen to the floor several times, even though the nail remained in the wall and the glass, unbroken, almost as if it had been placed on the floor rather than fallen.

But traffic rolling by could not explain the time they had locked up for the night, the picture hanging as normal, and upon their return the next morning, finding the portrait completely rotated on its longer-than-average hanging wire so that the prestigious Union general's countenance was turned, ignominiously, to face the wall.

14

THE BLUE LADY:
A CURSED WEEK ON
CHARLOTTE STREET

It was a strange week on Charlotte Street in May of 1974. The spate of unexplainable occurrences centered on the 500 block of Charlotte Street.

One account comes from author L. B. Taylor Jr. in his book, *Ghosts of Fredericksburg*, although I had the opportunity to interview the son of one of the witnesses to the unexplainable events, which add to the mystique of Fredericksburg.

A harbinger to the coming weirdness came one evening when the residents of Charlotte Street saw several Fredericksburg police cars gather outside of the Charlotte Street home of a woman who was employed the FBI. Leaving classified or even semi-classified government information out in the open is a serious federal crime, punishable by fines and prison time. Most federal employees are aware of this, and mindful of the grave consequences that await them if they fail to secure important government papers.

This woman kept some semi-classified documents in one of the upstairs rooms in her home which she habitually kept locked. She had gone upstairs to the room to work. When she unlocked the door she was stunned by what she saw. The place was ransacked: File cabinets were literally flipped and their contents tossed about the room. She frantically checked everything on the floor. In spite of the trashing of her office, not a single document had been removed. She was completely confused, she told the police. The windows also remained securely locked. How could anyone have entered or exited the locked room without leaving a window open, or at least, unlocked?

Another foreshadowing to the soon-to-come bizarre sightings was the strange entrance and exit of an invisible being from one of the nearby homes on the quiet residential street.

A woman was drying the lunch dishes one afternoon. From the front of the house, she distinctly heard the familiar sound of her screen door and front door opening. She thought it may have been her grandchildren coming for an unannounced visit, and called to them. No one answered. She walked to the living room, curious as to why the grandkids were being so uncharacteristically quiet. Upon entering the front room she realized that no one—at least, no one visible—had entered. Confused, but content to relegate the noises to her imagination, she returned to her dishes. A few seconds later, she heard the doors open again, this time in reverse order: the main door first, then the screen door, exactly as if whoever it was who had come for a visit was now leaving. Moving through her empty living room, she quickly exited the front door to try to see who it was, only to see that there was no one on the street anywhere near her home.

Yet another strange incident caught the woman's attention that same weird week in May of 1974. It was nighttime when she peered out her back window to observe what she described as an "amorphous form with a bluish cast" near Federal Hill, the imposing eighteenth-century mansion nearby. By its clearly shaped form she identified it as the figure of a woman. But it didn't walk like a normal, living woman. Instead, it floated above the ground as it neared Federal Hill. She made one other bizarre observation: To her horror, the blue woman was headless.

Again, during this month that seemed to have no end for those unfortunates living on Charlotte Street, the Lady in Blue was seen again, just a few doors down from the previous sightings.

It was a pleasant night. A resident of Charlotte Street was on his sunporch that night, watching television. As he stood up to change the channels (this was before widespread remote controls), he got that uneasy feeling he was being watched. He turned and, standing in his doorway, was the wispy form of a woman. She appeared to be from another time, in a dress that called to mind mid-nineteenth-century photographs he had seen. She emanated a blue glow that appeared to outline just her body, for, he observed, she was missing her head.

Confronted by such a strange sight in his own doorway, he felt like he'd stared at her for several minutes, yet admitted later that it couldn't have been more than a few seconds. According to the eyewitness, in a move that he felt showed her personality, she caught up the hemline of her dress in her hand, wrapped herself in the phantom cloth, and floated right past him. He watched as she passed through his dining room, then simply dematerialized. He rushed to the kitchen window and looked out. At Federal Hill, he caught sight of the bluish translucence that had just left his house, floating in the garden of the mansion, then slowly fading into the distance.

To this day, no one has been able to come up with a satisfactory explanation as to why that one week in May, 1974, could have been so supernaturally charged—unless it had something to do with the Civil War battles fought in Fredericksburg.

In December of 1862, Union artillery was set up in the yard of Federal Hill; in fact, remnants of their "lunettes," the crescent-shaped earthworks special to artillery, can still be seen there. One of the shots from the artillery stationed there was said to have been the one that hit Confederate general Thomas R. R. Cobb in the leg, severing the femoral artery and causing him to bleed to death on the famous Sunken Road.

Also, in May of 1863, Union troops passed Federal Hill in their successful assault on Marye's Heights during the Battle of Chancellorsville. While the time of year is closer for a coincidental haunting of Charlotte Street, documentary evidence of the death of a woman by decapitation is elusive.

15

ST. GEORGE'S
EPISCOPAL CHURCH

It might seem incongruous to say that a house of God could be cursed. But with four major battles taking place within a few miles, and every large public building commandeered by the surgeons as hospitals for the wounded, the churches of Fredericksburg, if not cursed in the supernatural sense, certainly were in a practical sense.

St. George's Episcopal Church on Princess Anne Street, established in 1732, boasts the oldest congregation in Fredericksburg. George Washington and his family would ferry across the Rappahannock every Sunday to attend services at the church when they lived at Ferry Farm.

The present St. George's Episcopal Church was built in 1849 upon the site of the original church. The current building is actually the third church to be built on the site of the original church, where the Washingtons worshipped. The oldest gravestone in the adjacent cemetery dates back to 1752. Buried here are some of Fredericksburg's most honored and historic citizens, including Col. John Dandridge, father of Martha Washington, and William Paul, John Paul Jones's brother.

During the Civil War, the church remained in service for both Union and Confederate soldiers, depending upon who occupied the city at the time. The pews had been permanently installed, rendering them unremovable by hospital orderlies or Union soldiers. Some pews in other churches in Fredericksburg were torn out for space, or cut up and used for firewood or as headboards for gravesites. The main sanctuary has hardly changed from the original, but side balconies were added after the Civil War. Three original Tiffany stained-glass windows are installed in the church.

The church was damaged in the Union bombardment of December, 1862. Confederates used the church during the great Christian revivals in the Confederate Army in 1863. In 1864, it was used as a hospital for casualties from the Battles of the Wilderness and Spotsylvania, several miles to the west.

During the Battle of Fredericksburg in December of 1862, the church was used by the Union Army as a hospital. One wounded Northerner described what he saw outside the building along the stairs: "dead soldiers piled on either side as high as the top step, and the fence hanging full of belts, cartridge boxes, canteens, and haversacks." The fence and the steps currently associated with the church are the originals.

But it is what has been seen *inside* the church that most interests ghost hunters. And not all of the ghost stories from the church originate with the Civil War.

The original story, found in *Virginia Ghosts* by Marguerite DuPont Lee, relates that several years before war came to Fredericksburg, in 1858, a local girl named Miss Ella McCarty was a singer in the choir of St. George's. She had arrived at the church one night with a gentleman and found that they were early. The church was still dark, and only the male organist was present. The two men left Miss McCarty sitting in the church, which was lit by one candle in the choir loft (then located over the vestibule), while they looked for more candles. As she sat and her eyes grew accustomed to the dark, she saw a female figure that appeared to be dressed all in white, with a veil over her face, kneeling at the rail in the front of the church. The woman in white was apparently in prayer, and within a short time, she arose and, almost as if she were floating, turned to face Miss McCarty. She looked at her with a forlorn, desperate expression. Trying to be polite, Miss McCarty began to speak to her, but the woman vanished.

Fast-forward to the twenty-first century. A young woman was in the church and went into the restroom. From inside one of the stalls she heard the door to the restroom open and the door to the next stall open. Moments later, when she was leaving, she began to realize something strange. Although she had heard someone walk into the restroom, walk across the floor, and open the stall door, she hadn't heard anyone leave, and there was no one in the room with her. Cautiously, she pushed open the stall door and realized that, in spite of the footsteps she had heard, she had been alone in the room the entire time.

Also, according to the local police, their K-9 police dogs are unexplainably nervous inside and outside of the church. The dogs especially react at the door to the balcony. "There aren't too many police officers who haven't had an experience in St. George's," said one officer. Fredericksburg police officers, as part of their patrol duties, will check the doors of the church at night to make sure they are locked—and they are. An hour or so later, they'll check again and they will be unlocked. Officers will sometimes hear footsteps walking through the sanctuary when they are alone in the church; sometimes they will hear the benches creaking as if someone was sitting in them. The caretaker was once working in the cemetery and felt someone come up behind him and touch him on the shoulder, but when he turned around to see what the person wanted, there was no one there.

But one of the strangest things that ever occurred in the church happened recently to two local police officers. A veteran cop and a rookie were on patrol one night. They had already checked the doors at St. George's once, and found them locked, but knowing their reputation, had stopped again to check the doors.

"I'll get this," volunteered the rookie.

The veteran officer watched as he climbed the stone stairs, once slick with gore from hundreds of wounded soldiers. Sure enough, as if someone was too busy carrying wounded in and out to bother with them, the doors were unlocked. The rookie gestured to the veteran, indicating that he would inspect inside the church to make sure no one was there, and entered.

Several minutes passed. Then several more. Enough time had passed that the veteran cop was getting concerned about his partner. Just as he was about to leave the car to check on him, the rookie appeared at the door and locked it. Upon returning to the car, he reported that everything in the church looked fine.

"I checked everything," he told his superior proudly. Then he said something that surprised the veteran. "Even that weird room that's painted all red."

There was only one problem: There is no red room in St. George's Episcopal Church.

16

CURSED CRIME SCENES: BELLE GROVE PLANTATION AND AQUIA CHURCH

BELLE GROVE PLANTATION

As I have learned from co-writing two books on crime scenes, they can be cursed and haunted by the ghosts of victims, witnesses, and sometimes others, innocent of any involvement.

Belle Grove Plantation near Middletown is located south of Winchester. It was designed in part by Thomas Jefferson, and finished in 1797. The end result of Jefferson's design was a magnificent mansion over one hundred feet in length. The plantation itself was begun in 1783, by a former American officer in the Revolutionary War, Maj. Isaac Hite Jr., after he married Nelly Conway Madison, sister of the future president James Madison. Madison visited the plantation several times, even spending part of his honeymoon there. After his first wife's death, the major married Ann Tunstall Maury. They added ten more children to the three from the major's first marriage. Uncommonly for the time, all survived to adulthood but one. Adding to his holdings and building upon the fruits of his imagination, Hite saw the plantation grow, eventually enlarging it to contain a large stone smokehouse with a fine flagstone path leading to it, an icehouse, and slave quarters. He also owned a sawmill, general store, distillery, and gristmill in the vicinity. Upon his and Ann's deaths, Belle Grove was sold out of the Hite family.

Then came the Civil War. By that time Benjamin Coolie (or Cooley) was living at Belle Grove. Coolie owned slaves. One, a feisty young woman named Harriette Robinson, was apparently more to Coolie than just his cook and housekeeper. As a house servant, she was in close proximity to the master of the house at all times of the day and night, and enjoyed an easier lifestyle than the slaves that worked the fields.

Marguerite DuPont Lee, in *Virginia Ghosts*, wrote that Harriette was overheard saying that if a mistress were ever to come to the house, her days would be numbered. Perhaps he never even knew of the threat, or foolishly thought it an idle boast, but Coolie did take a wife. As Harriette and the new mistress of the house began to interact, there were fireworks. The servant was blatant in disregarding the new Mrs. Coolie's authority. L. B. Taylor Jr. in *The Ghosts of Virginia*, recorded that the hostility was so vitriolic that Mrs. Coolie asked her husband to sell Harriette. For reasons that can only be speculated upon, Coolie did not.

The minor quarrels eventually grew in intensity, from disobedience to back talk to physical punishments. Over a missing stocking, Mrs. Coolie beat Harriette with a broomstick. Unaccustomed to harsh treatment and seething anyway over her displacement in the affections of the man of the plantation, Harriette chose her moment and struck back. One day Mrs. Coolie was giving orders to Harriette in the cellar of the main house. Harriette objected, grabbed a nearby ax, and split her tormentor's skull. Harriette then dragged her body down the lovely flagstone path and threw her half-dead rival into the smokehouse. Some of the other slaves witnessed Harriette leaving the smokehouse and investigated.

They were astounded. The attacks upon the incapacitated mistress had continued in the smokehouse. She had fingernail marks on her throat after being choked, and her cheekbone was shattered. The two gashes on her forehead were deep enough to expose the bone, and she had been punched repeatedly in her face; when found, her feet were burning in the smokehouse fire. But she still lived.

She regained consciousness. Perhaps fearful of a retaliatory attack, or perhaps a threat to her husband made by the vindictive Harriette, she said that her injuries were caused by herself: She had simply fallen. When questioned directly, she refused to implicate Harriette. To all who saw her, it was obvious that her injuries were so severe, a fall as the cause was out of the question. Shedding no more light upon the crime, Mrs. Coolie died a few days later.

In spite of Mrs. Coolie's refusal to name her killer, Harriette was arrested.

The circumstantial evidence against Harriette was overwhelming. Numerous people had heard the threats upon the victim's life. There were all the previous altercations, both verbal and physical, and the dress Harriette washed right after the assault, as if she were covering up evidence. Another slave testified that she had been asked by Harriette for some poison, and had heard the words of a scorned woman: Harriette said she didn't care if they caught her and hanged her; she would "have my revenge!"

With not a single sign of remorse, Harriette was tried, convicted, and sentenced. But she still beat the hangman.

While awaiting her execution, L. B. Taylor Jr. documented that she died in prison. Another version, told by Marguerite DuPont Lee, is that while she was jailed, the Yankees rolled through the Shenandoah Valley and released all the prisoners in the jail. Whichever version is true, Harriette Robinson vanished. "Ever since," wrote Lee, "the ghost of Mrs. Coolie has walked."

Testimony comes from the Rose family, who occupied the house twenty-some years after the murder. They often saw the same ghost roaming the grounds. Lee recorded their experiences in *Virginia Ghosts*. One of the things they reported seeing was a white figure in the basement, standing by the fireplace. Unnervingly, it would float along the very flagstone path down which Mrs. Coolie had been dragged, to the smokehouse. The white specter would also show up in the hallway of the mansion, or gaze at visitors outside from the windows.

The current owners emphasize the rich history of the plantation rather than its ghosts. But at least one tour guide has had a number of supernatural experiences which may or may not be associated with Harriette.

"Women in white" are relatively common apparitions at many haunted sites. At Belle Grove, however, a woman in black has been seen in one of the upper windows. A possible explanation could come from the fact that Belle Grove is on the 1864 Civil War Battlefield of Cedar Creek. The psychic remnant of a woman in mourning for a dead relative would not be out of place.

Then there was the UPS man who arrived to deliver a package. A little girl with cute blonde curls answered the door and let him in, then ran upstairs. At that moment, the resident entered the house and inquired of the delivery man how he had gained entry; she had locked the door when she left. He told her that her little daughter had let him in. The woman told him that she had no daughter.

He left, seemingly in a hurry, and the woman searched in vain for the small, golden-haired child, without success. Some have an explanation, though. They point to the fact that the first owners, Major and Mrs. Hite, did have that one child who, because of unknown circumstances, never really had the chance to grow up.

AQUIA CHURCH

There are people who believe that churches cannot be cursed, yet there is a blessed structure that seems to have been cursed nearly from the day it was first built.

Aquia Church, according to those who live in the area, is one of the more haunted sites between the Rappahannock and Potomac Rivers, north of Fredericksburg. Construction of the original Aquia Church was completed in 1751. Much of it was destroyed by fire in 1755. Construction on the second and current church was completed in 1757. During the time of the American Revolution, the murder of a young woman was committed on the very floor under which early parishioners are buried to await the great and glorious Resurrection Day. For nearly two hundred years one of the flagstones in the floor of the center aisle of the church was stained with the blood of the young woman killed in the sanctuary. Can you imagine what went through the minds of the faithful as they bent their heads in prayer and peeped through slitted eyes at the gory stains on their aisle floor? It was finally covered over in later years by cement.

After the murder, the unknown perpetrator (or perpetrators) secreted the body in the belfry. Sometime after the murder, the church was abandoned and the body went undetected for a number of years. When it was finally discovered, there was nothing left but a bleached skeleton with long blonde hair still attached to a gruesomely grinning skull.

For many years it has been rumored that not even the bravest citizens of Stafford County have been able to force themselves, as the clock approaches midnight, to approach and enter Aquia Church. It is rumored that this is when the sounds begin.

Those who merely walk past the church in the night have reported the noises emanating from the church's interior. They are described as "heavy" noises, much like a struggle or fight is going on inside—sounds that might not be so unnerving, if it wasn't for the horrid, rumored history of the church that everyone knows. Strangely, the noises are said to immediately cease once someone is courageous enough to enter.

On an undocumented date before the 1930s, before there were paranormal investigators or ghost hunters, a woman interested in the supernatural as a hobby decided that any evidence of the haunting of Aquia Church should be documented for posterity's sake. She wanted to investigate at midnight, since that is when the activity was rumored to be at its peak. Recruiting help from the locals proved impossible; they'd all heard—and some had even experienced—the strange, frightening, unexplainable noises associated with the house of worship.

She finally got the help of two individuals from Washington, DC, experts in sound and audio recording. They would document any auditory anomalies should they happen. They got to the church just before the clock struck midnight. Just as the woman crossed the threshold of the church she was slapped hard across the face. Her companions heard the sharp slap and her scream of surprise and pain and ran to see what had happened. They also realized that whoever had slapped the woman did it with a hand that was invisible, for no one else, apart from the investigators, was discovered in the church that night. The investigation, with the escalation to violence, was abruptly called off, but the mark of the phantom hand remained on the woman's face for days afterwards.

Around the same early-twentieth-century time period, the rumors of strange, violent noises coming from the church at midnight were augmented by persistent reports of sightings of a young, blonde woman, hair trailing down beyond her shoulders, looking out the windows of the church. Her description was reminiscent of the woman allegedly murdered in the sanctuary. Some of the men in the neighborhood were tired of all the superstitious nonsense and decided to prove, once and for all, that their neighbors were idiots. We know that there were at least three of them, because once they got to the church in the dead of night, only one was brave enough to enter the church. One can imagine the scene as one of the men berated the others for their timidity. *He* was not afraid. *He* would go into the church by himself and climb to the belfry alone.

His friends were suspicious of his courage. He would probably just go inside the door, wait a few minutes, then come out bragging. He rummaged in the back of his truck and took out a hammer and nail. He would pound the nail into the wood of the belfry, then, when they were brave enough—in broad daylight, maybe—they could climb to the belfry and see for themselves the proof that he had visited the dreaded site where the body had been hidden.

Inside he went. His friends laughed nervously. Ten minutes passed. Twenty went by, and they began to worry. They called to him to come out. He can quit fooling around, now. It's not funny anymore. More time passed, and his friends began to get worried.

Had he injured himself? Was he incapacitated and in need of their help? After an hour, their concern for their friend began to overcome their fear of the unknown. They got some lanterns from the truck and entered the church. They looked around the church but couldn't find him. Reluctantly, they started to climb to the belfry. When they reached the top, what they saw shocked them.

He was there, eyes open and staring, his mouth frozen in a silent scream, hammer next to him. He was dead. Moving the lantern closer, they saw that, in the dark, he had unknowingly hammered the nail through his own coat. As he had tried to leave, it must have felt as if something unseen had grabbed him. He pulled but it wouldn't release him. Believing now in the evil that lived in the church, his heart gave out and he died of fright.

One more story comes from Aquia Church, this time from the annals of the Civil War. William Fitzhugh was a Confederate cavalryman from Fredericksburg. He and another Rebel soldier had been scouting for Yankees in the vicinity of the church in Aquia. Night came on before they made it back to their camp. They were exhausted and so, in spite of the haunted reputation of the church, they decided to spend the night inside. They were to be the victims of what is known as a "harbinger," in modern paranormal parlance.

They curled up in their blankets on the hard pews and fell asleep. It would prove to be a restless night. Shortly after midnight they were both awakened by the sound of shuffling feet echoing off the flagstone aisle in the center of the church. They remained hunkered down behind the pew backs. Were they about to be captured by Yankees? Then they heard it: a soft whistling floating through the church. It was a tune they were soon to recognize, from Fitzhugh's ancestral home of the British Isles. Wafting through the sanctuary was the ancient Scottish war melody, "The Campbells Are Coming." As suddenly as it had begun, the whistling stopped. The two young men looked at each other. The whistling began again, this time closer to them. Then it stopped. Another few seconds passed, and again, nearly next to them came the whistling: *The Campbells are coming, Hurrah! Hurrah!*

They leapt from the pews and struck a match to confront whoever it was, right next to them. The flaring light revealed . . . no one.
But from outside on the road they heard the rattle of horses' hooves
and military commands shouted in a decidedly Northern accent.
Having had the advantage of being awakened by the helpful phantom's whistling, they were able to exit through the back windows,
mount their horses, and ride to safety, convinced ever after that they
had been saved by a ghost.

17

CHANCELLORSVILLE: A CURSED VICTORY

The spring of 1863 brought new life to the military successes of the Confederacy. The Battle of Fredericksburg, fought the past December, was an unmitigated Federal disaster, with thousands of young men in blue hurled time and again against impregnable Confederate positions. Union losses far outnumbered Confederate casualties, and Confederates maintained their positions on the ground they had chosen.

At the beginning of the New Year, Union commander Ambrose Burnside decided to pursue a flank march to get around the Southerners and dislodge them from their position. Winter weather turned his "flank" march into a much-derided "mud" march, and the Confederates maintained their positions between Washington and Richmond. Burnside was also out of a job, replaced by Maj. Gen. Joseph Hooker.

As soon as Hooker took command, he reorganized the army and came up with a plan for a spring offensive, created to drive Lee from his Fredericksburg entrenchments.

Hooker ordered ten thousand fast-moving cavalrymen on a ride southward to cut Lee's communications with Richmond. With the Union cavalry forcing Lee to worry for his capital, some of Hooker's infantry would also distract Lee with an attack upon Confederates on Marye's Heights, behind Fredericksburg. The majority of Hooker's army would then march up the north side of the Rappahannock River, cross, and fall on Lee's left and rear.

Lee had already weakened his own army during the winter lull in the fighting by sending Gen. James Longstreet and his troops south to bring supplies for his army to Virginia. Lee left himself with only 60,000 men to contest some 130,000 Federal troops bent on his destruction. By the end of April, Hooker was on the move, crossing Maj. Gen. John Sedgwick's Sixth Corps at Fredericksburg, threatening Lee with a successful attack on his weakened defenses on Marye's Heights. In the meantime, some 40,000 Union troops were fording the Rappahannock upriver. Lee, his army in a tenuous trap, performed his trademark move: rather than retreat, he attacked.

By the afternoon of April 30, 1863, Hooker's fifty thousand troops, accompanied by one hundred pieces of artillery, had crossed the Rappahannock at fords, broke out of the tangled Wilderness, and arrived at the Chancellorsville crossroads. But instead of pressing the advantage Hooker halted, waiting for more of his soldiers to arrive.

Thomas J. "Stonewall" Jackson, of First Manassas fame, after riding through the night of May 1, arrived on the battlefield and impetuously ordered the first Confederates he found to attack the Yankees. The move forced Hooker's hand and his plans crumbled. He ordered his men to fall back to a defensive position in the Wilderness. After planning a brilliant tactical offensive, Hooker was intimidated into taking a defensive position.

That evening, at the intersection of the Plank Road and Furnace Road, in this forlorn area of Virginia, two of history's greatest commanders met. Sitting on discarded hardtack crates, they planned what many military historians have called the perfect tactical battle. For Robert E. Lee it would lead to a brilliant victory; for Stonewall Jackson, it would carry him to his death; for the Confederacy, it would toll its doom.

Confederate cavalry commander, Maj. Gen. J. E. B. Stuart, had returned from a scouting mission and relayed the information that Hooker's right flank was "in the air"; it was not fortified to any great extent. Jackson proposed that he take a force on a looping march and strike the Federals hard on that exposed flank. Fortunately for Lee, some Confederates in his army had been born and raised in the area of Fredericksburg and the Wilderness. They were consulted, and confirmed that there was a little-used dirt byway that would lead directly to the Federals' right flank.

Sitting on his cracker box, Lee asked Jackson how many men he proposed to take on this risky march to the Union flank. Jackson replied that he would take his entire corps—nearly three-quarters of Lee's entire army. Lee would be committing a military faux pas, splitting his army in the face of an active enemy. Jackson would leave Lee with only 14,000 men to hold off Hooker's entire army. Lee pondered, weighing the dangers if Hooker attacked while Jackson was on his march. Such was his faith in Jackson that he then gave the orders to his trusted subordinate to begin his preparations for the march.

Early that morning of May 2, Jackson's men were on the march. Lee and Jackson spoke on horseback one more time. It would their last earthly meeting.

Jackson's men ate dust all day, marching along a little-used local "road" through the woods. Finally, by 5:00 p.m., after a hot, dry, twelve-mile march, Stonewall was ready. On the Federals' extreme right flank, the men of the Federal Eleventh Corps lounged about, cooked meals, and relaxed, with their weapons stacked. It was nearing dusk, and fighting for the day seemed over; during the Civil War, because field communications depended a great deal on daylight to succeed, battles rarely took place after dark.

So Jackson's corps faced only two unsuspecting Union regiments and a few cannon pointed in their direction.

From the thick woods to the west of the Union position burst rabbits, deer, and other small game, stampeding through the Union camps. Then the darkening woods echoed the staccato call of bugles and the yipping Rebel yell, followed by wild-looking armed men charging into the Federal campsites. Some Yankees attempted to hold, but all were swept away. The Union Eleventh Corps disintegrated, running back into its own main army, sowing panic and fear as it went.

By 7:15 p.m., Jackson's attack had lost momentum. In the darkening woods, Jackson intended to renew his attack as soon as he could reorganize. His desire was to cut off the Yankees from the river fords and safety. Maj. Gen. A. P. Hill's division was prepared to renew the fight. As they were replacing the worn-out troops, about 9:00 p.m., Jackson and his staff rode out in the darkness in front of the lines to reconnoiter. He had found the Federal line and was returning when a North Carolina regiment, skittish at the sound of horses' hooves coming at them from the direction of the enemy, fired at what they thought was Yankee cavalry. It was Jackson's scouting party. Stonewall was hit by three bullets, and under Federal fire, carried off the field. Cavalryman J. E. B. Stuart was called from his duties to command Jackson's infantry. Because of his unfamiliarity with the terrain and the difficulty in launching a night assault, he postponed Jackson's planned attack until daylight.

The fighting at Chancellorsville continued the next day while Jackson was taken to the rear. At Wilderness Tavern, his wounds were attended to, including the amputation of his mangled left arm two inches below the shoulder. He then endured a twenty-seven-mile wagon ride to Guinea Station on the Richmond, Fredericksburg and Petersburg Railroad. From there, when he recovered, they hoped he would be transported to the capital for a full recovery, to rejoin the Confederacy in her fight for independence.

His wife and infant daughter came to Guinea Station, and for a while Jackson seemed to be recovering. But the hardships of living and fighting while exposed to the elements took their toll on the wounded man. He contracted pneumonia, faded quickly, and died on Sunday, May 10, 1863.

Lee's victory at Chancellorsville is written in the annals of military history as one of the most audacious ever achieved. Outnumbered and outgunned, he split his army three times before an enemy and still gained victory. It was momentous enough to allow him to conceive of another invasion of the Northern states just a month later. Perhaps it gave him too much confidence. The invasion ended at Gettysburg, which he had to fight without Jackson, a curse he could not overcome.

18

THE CURSED
WILDERNESS

All circumstances seemed to combine to make the scene one of unutterable horror.
It was as though Christian men had turned to fiends,
and hell itself has usurped the place of earth.

—Lt. Col. Horace Porter, Ulysses S. Grant's Staff,
writing about the Battle of the Wilderness

Beginning several miles to the west of Fredericksburg, as the flood-plain of the Rappahannock levels out, is a seventy-square-mile area of Virginia called "the Wilderness." In the twenty-first century, one can drive through it in less than an hour on well-paved and cared-for highways. There are campgrounds, paved two-lane roads through the National Park holdings, and a few areas of residential development. But just off the roads and beyond the developments, the woods get thick, the underbrush tangled; vines grab at a person's ankles and the air ceases to move. Without a compass in some places it would be easy to get lost, especially if you were visiting, like many of the officers and soldiers who fought there, for the first time. Darkness makes moving through the tangle nearly impossible.

When the Federal and Confederate armies made war there, in 1863, during the Battle of Chancellorsville, and again in 1864, during the Battles of the Wilderness and Spotsylvania, the area became a virtual participant in the fighting.

Lee, knowing his artillery was outnumbered by the powerful Federals, wanted to draw them into the area and thereby nullify any numerical advantage they might have. The Federal commanders—in particular, Maj. Gen. Joseph Hooker, and later, Ulysses Grant—wanted to clear their armies from the gloomy woods onto open ground as quickly as possible.

The Wilderness provided cover to attacking forces when the smoke from battle hovered in the airless atmosphere under its canopy of trees; its fallen logs provided ready-cut breastworks for defenders to hide behind and obstacles to slow up attackers; and it offered up a horrifying death when it caught fire and consumed alive those wounded and unable to crawl from its inexorably advancing flames. Of all places associated with the American Civil War, it probably still embraces the bodies—or what is left of them—of the slain, hastily buried after the battles, then forgotten, in that most forlorn of all places in Virginia that is still a wilderness.

The Battle of the Wilderness, May 5–6, 1864, had all the elements the ancient Greeks believed activated their myths: water in the form of the Rapidan River and Wilderness Run; fire, which would engulf parts of the woods, burning the dead and living alike; and air, that soon filled with choking smoke from the burning pine trees, underbrush, and the slowly roasting bodies of men and animals.

The worst of all these was the fire.

In the spring of 1864, Gen. Robert E. Lee and his Confederate Army of Northern Virginia waited across the Rapidan River, a tributary to the Rappahannock, for the Federal Army of the Potomac. Lee was in no hurry to fight, since a large part of his army—Longstreet's Corps—was not with him. Gen. Ulysses Grant had been made commander of all the armies of the North, but had chosen to headquarter with the Army of the Potomac. Though the Army of the Potomac was commanded directly by Maj. Gen. George G. Meade, of Gettysburg fame, the names of Grant and Lee would be linked imperishably in history.

Lee, without Longstreet, was vastly outnumbered, and realized that his only deliverance would be to fight Grant in the tangled, wooded area of this part of Virginia, nullifying the North's numerical superiority in men and artillery, and stalling them until Longstreet arrived. It was as if the Wilderness itself would become a player in the great battle.

On May 4, 1864, the Union Army began crossing the Rapidan, looking to go around Lee's right flank, then head south. The Union command believed the Confederates to be miles away. When Meade got word that Lee was near, he halted his advance through the woods to confront him. Lee's battle plan of catching the enemy in the Wilderness was working.

Only three roads run west to east, parallel to each other through the Wilderness: the Orange Turnpike, the Orange Plank Road, and Catharpin Road. The Brock Road runs north to south along the eastern edge of what would soon be the battlefield. Should the Confederates advance along any of the three parallel roads and gain the Brock Road, they would have cut the Union Army into pieces. But, outmanned, they were forced to fight cautiously.

With the infantry marching on the few, poor, winding roads through thick woods, cavalry scouting ahead was vital to avoid deadly surprises from the enemy. Yet that was just what Meade was lacking. The Union cavalry assigned to patrol the front of the Union advance through the Wilderness had not been heard from since they'd left the main body early in the morning. They had run into Confederate cavalry and infantry marching eastward on the Orange Plank Road. When the fighting ended, the Union cavalry was effectively out of the battle.

By midday, Confederate general Richard Ewell had entrenched his 10,000 men along the western side of Saunders Field, stretching out on either side of the Orange Turnpike. They were backed by another 4,500 men in reserve. Lee's orders were to avoid battle until Longstreet arrived on the field, so they could only observe as columns of Yankee foot soldiers wound their way across their front. In the distance to the south, smoke was already rising ominously from fires along the Orange Plank Road, set when Union cavalrymen abandoned their campfires to engage.

Lee himself had advanced along the Orange Plank Road behind Hill's infantry, and, with his renowned cavalry commander J. E. B.

Stuart and Gen. A. P. Hill, stopped at the Widow Tapp's farm. There, he nervously awaited the arrival of Longstreet's Corps.

In the meantime, Grant established his headquarters, along with Meade, at "Ellwood," summer home of J. Horace Lacy of Fredericksburg's "Chatham" Manor. With the appearance of Grant at his headquarters, the Federals' battle plan was energized, and a race began for the junction of the Brock and Orange Plank Roads. If Confederates gained the crossroads, the Union Army would be blocked from further advance.

A Union general and his staff arrived at the crossroads ahead of their troops. As they sat on their horses awaiting their men, in the distance, on the Orange Plank Road, they could see misty forms approaching. From that direction a bullet zipped . . . then another . . . then a dozen. The small group of mounted officers stood their ground in the intersection, taking enemy fire and waiting. Suddenly, from down the Brock Road came figures in blue. They swarmed into the crossroads, cut loose a volley to hold the approaching Confederates, and the general and his staff, miraculously with only one man wounded, withdrew to safer ground. When Union skirmishers pushed out, they found wounded Confederates only thirty yards from the Brock Road. The race had been that close.

Finally, six hours after Meade had ordered it, Union troops began their advance west on the Orange Turnpike in an attack against Ewell's dug-in Confederates. Confusion reigned almost immediately: thornbushes, scrub brush, and tangled thickets grabbed at ankles. In some areas the trees were so thick commanders, in desperation, pulled out pocket compasses to guide them through the jungle. An occasional company would have to narrow to single file to pass a particularly dense growth of briars. Just before 1:00 p.m., the Union assault reached the open terrain of Saunders Field. The large force Meade wanted attacking the Confederates had dissolved into a much smaller force—one-quarter the size—for the assault. The Wilderness, like some unseen force, seemed to be orchestrating the battle and devouring manpower.

Halfway across Saunders Field is a gully that cuts the field diagonally. As soon as Union troops crossed it, officers in the rear sent two pieces of artillery down the Orange Turnpike and across a crude wooden bridge over the gully, to set up in support of the advance. Exposed in the center of the road, they were fired on by Confederate sharpshooters perched in trees. Artillery horses screamed as they were struck and men tumbled as they attempted to work the guns. The artillerists aimed the cannons at an angle from the road and began firing at the Confederate line. Unfortunately, their own troops were between them and the enemy. The Union artillery won no friends in the infantry this day.

Coming on the heels of the initial Federal assault was the 146th New York Regiment. They were still wearing brightly colored Zouave uniforms, throwbacks to the early days of the war when it was part game, part fashion show, illustrating the latest style worn by French troops in the 1850s in Morocco. As they reached the gully, they made conspicuous targets for the Confederates, who were, after three years of war, much better shots than in 1861. Many a Zouave crumpled in the field.

Other Union troops to the right of the Zouaves found the fighting in the area almost impossible, if not otherworldly: When they could be seen, the Rebels in their gray and butternut uniforms moving through the black-powder smoke looked more like ghosts than men, and the bursts of yellow from muzzles illuminated the scene as if it were Hell. Organized unit combat became nonexistent and battles devolved upon handfuls of men. The Federals finally broke for the rear, except for two Union regiments—including the Zouaves—which clung to the earth in front of the Confederate line.

Farther to the south, other Federal units—including the Iron Brigade of South Mountain and Gettysburg fame—attacked the entrenched Confederate line. They ran into another unit made famous by Gettysburg, Brig. Gen. John B. Gordon's Georgians. The famed Iron Brigade broke, and the Confederates advanced toward the Lacy House, capturing scores of prisoners, before halting their advance.

Even farther south along the Federal attack, the Union assault bogged down—literally—in a swamp near the Higgerson Farm. The units slogged waist-deep in water until they veered off in divergent directions. More than one soldier believed their officers were drunk. To their left, other Union troops ran into Confederates in a hollow in the ground, retreated, and left bodies piled in the depression.

The "butcher's bill"—Civil War parlance for casualty lists—was horrifying. Saunders Field filled with dead and dying humans and horses; those who could crawl made it to the gully and lay down, Union and Confederate side by side, hunkered down with faces to the earth to avoid the crossfire from both sides. The 146th New York took an incredible 46 percent casualties; the Zouaves of the 140th suffered 51 percent killed, wounded, and missing. But then, as bad as things were, they got immeasurably worse.

Fiery discharges from Rebel rifle-muskets lit the dry tinder in Saunders Field on fire. The field south of the Pike became an inferno, and the wounded that could, attempted to crawl from the scorching flames. Those who couldn't move burned alive within view of their comrades, who could not get to them because of the heat. When the fire died, the living noticed weird, charred, smoldering lumps throughout the field—the remains of those cremated alive in the holocaust. By 2:30 p.m. the Union attacks in Saunders Field, like the fires, had died out, failures because of the piecemeal fashion in which they were made.

Later, to stall the Yankee attacks, Confederates purposefully set the woods on fire. This second round of fighting ended around 4:00 p.m., leaving the smoky cauldron of the Wilderness the only winner.

Meanwhile, General Meade ordered an advance along the Orange Plank Road from the Brock Road at 4:15. Mounted upon his horse, Union general Alexander Hays began to address one of his regiments for inspiration. The powerful speech was ended by the odd thump of a bullet smashing into his skull. The lofty thoughts and ringing words muted by that clod of metal will remain forever floating in the weird air of the Wilderness.

Confederates were again approaching the vital Brock Road–Orange Plank Road intersection by 4:45. Union general Winfield Hancock, bullets whistling past him while he sat his horse at the crossroads, gave orders to retreating units to re-form, and called upon his own men to hurry to the endangered road crossing. The Confederates were within seconds of seizing the Brock Road, when Hancock's foremost units launched themselves into the smoldering trees, pushing the enemy back.

Shortly after 5:00 p.m. a Rebel prisoner would cough up information that would affect the Union battle plan for the rest of May 5 and part of May 6. He intimated to his captors that Longstreet's Corps was fast approaching the Confederate right flank. Hancock's troops had just left open the intersection of the Brock and Catharpin Roads; should Longstreet capture it, he would have free access to the entire Union left and rear. In reality, Longstreet was well behind his scheduled arrival on the battlefield, but without cavalry, the only information the Union command had was from the prisoner.

In the meantime, however, the Orange Plank Road had become so dangerous (because of flying lead) that to cross it would be suicidal. The two armies, forced into a face-to-face slugfest by the Wilderness, attacked, countered, and blasted away at what appeared to be mere phantoms, materializing and disappearing in the drifting smoke. Some Confederates found refuge behind Yankees, killed earlier in such quantities as to have their dead bodies used as breastworks.

Around 6:00 p.m., Union assaults on the Orange Plank Road against the Rebels renewed. At 6:30 the final Confederate reinforcements were brought in to try to stem the tide. One North Carolina unit they relieved posted casualty figures: In the three hours of fighting they had lost an astonishing 59 percent; before them lay 157 dead of the enemy.

Grant had determined correctly that there must be a gap between Ewell's dug-in Corps and Hill's, and began to take advantage of it. As Union troops drove toward the gap, only 150 men from the 5th Alabama had remained un-blooded. The unit was so small that it was being used to guard prisoners. The tiny group charged, screaming the Rebel yell at the top of their lungs. In the dusky, smoky, confusing forest of the Wilderness, they apparently sounded like a massive assault. The attacking Federals stopped and fired blindly, their forward impetus blunted. The fighting along the Orange Plank Road died with the light. The two opposing lines were a few score yards apart, close enough to hear each other digging in, their talking echoing eerily in the ghostly woods.

While the fighting along the Orange Plank Road progressed into the waning daylight, the battle to the north, along the Orange Turnpike, flared again.

Union assault upon that flank failed and those woods caught on fire. And while the overwhelming weight of Union artillery was somehow negated by the terrain and foliage of the Wilderness, Confederate artillery fired down the Turnpike, filling the air with shells and bouncing solid shot off the ground and into the air. One round exploded inside a soldier, gutting him and launching his body, spinning like a hideous whirligig, over the heads of his fellow soldiers, raining upon them bits of flesh, intestines, and blood.

By 10:00 p.m., the firing along the lines had died. As the sounds of battle subsided, they were replaced by the mournful moans of the wounded. The Wilderness, once again, played a merciless role in the agony of the common soldier. All through the night the survivors of the day could hear the cries for help of the wounded and the ominous crackling of the fires creeping closer and closer to them. The groans grew louder and more panicked, then became piercing shrieks as the flames burned the wounded to death. The smoke, the moonless darkness illuminated only by the lurid, flickering fires, and the screams and pleadings of the victims until they were consumed, certainly recalled among many a soldier his own image of a personal and all too intimate Hell.

From Ellwood, Grant sent orders to gather every available man in the ranks—engineers, guards, and artillerymen, whose weapons were nullified by the Wilderness—for a final assault on the Confederate lines. He planned to attack Confederates on the Turnpike and on the Orange Plank Road. Previously unused troops under Gen. Ambrose Burnside, of Fredericksburg infamy, would rush between the two advancing columns toward the Confederate center and divide Lee's army.

For Lee there was nothing to do but wait impatiently for Longstreet to arrive. In the face of the overwhelming Federal superiority, the fate of his army, and perhaps the life of the Confederacy, depended upon it.

At 5:00 a.m., May 6, Grant's attack began. Expecting to be relieved by Longstreet during the night, the Rebels had not built breastworks or entrenchments. The result of a massive assault against unentrenched troops was predictable. The Confederates were driven all the way back to Lee's headquarters at Widow Tapp's Farm. To slow the Northerners' fire, Rebels propped wounded Union soldiers up against trees between them and the advancing troops so the Federals would not fire in the direction of their own men. The tactic worked.

By a quarter past five, Union troops were driving the Confederates back on the Orange Plank Road, but there was no sign of the Yankees' center force. Another Union attack from the north upon the Orange Plank Road did materialize, but they got intermingled with their own troops attacking from the east and merely added to the confusion.

Union troops reached the edge of the Widow Tapp's fields. There they were greeted by a dozen Southern cannon, shells slicing across the Orange Plank Road. But numbers favored the Federal troops. Lee's cannoneers were only buying time, and both sides knew it. Yankees curled around the edges of Lee's men. Each minute seemed to ring the death knell of Lee's Army of Northern Virginia.

Then, from behind Widow Tapp's Farm, having marched an unbelievable thirty-two miles in twenty-four hours, came Longstreet's First Corps. Exhaustion was now an afterthought. They marched past other Confederates streaming to the rear, and realized then that they were saving Lee's army from certain destruction.

One of Longstreet's units in particular caught the eye of General Lee. Eight hundred Texans under Brig. Gen. John Gregg hurriedly formed into line near him. Lee asked what troops they were, and was told, the Texas Brigade. Lee expressed his pleasure at that information. He declared that the Texans always drive the enemy, and wanted every man to know that he was watching their conduct. Gregg called the brigade to attention and told them, "The eyes of General Lee are upon you! Forward. March."

Neither Lee nor the men could control their emotions. The Texans let out a cheer; Lee waved his hat and cried, "Texans always move them!" A member of the brigade, about to face near-certain death, his eyes welling with tears, declared, "I would charge Hell itself for that old man."

Overcome by the knowledge that his army was about to be saved, his military blood up, Lee himself rode out to lead the charge. The Texans would have none of it. They might die in the next few minutes, but not General Lee. They shouted that they would not go on unless Lee returned to the rear. Gnarled, sunburned hands grabbed his reins and tried to turn his horse. Longstreet himself rode up and assured Lee that he could stop the enemy. Lee, regaining his composure, rode to the rear.

For the honor of fighting under the eyes of Lee, the Texans paid dearly. With no support on the flanks, they marched into an old-fashioned, stand-up fight with an overwhelming number of Federals, just twenty yards away. Rolling volleys and firing at will continued for twenty-five long minutes. When the Texans finally withdrew they left nearly 70 percent of their number—some 550 Lone Star soldiers—marking the area where they had stood, fought, and died. But they honored their promise to General Lee and stopped the Yankee advance.

More of Longstreet's brigades entered the fight. Georgians joined the Texans, then Alabamians. An attacking Union soldier thought the scene resembled something from the most chaotic regions of Dante's Inferno. But by the time Longstreet's counterattack had lost its momentum, both Union assaults—from the east and the north—were blunted.

Along the Orange Turnpike to the north Grant's planned 5:00 a.m. attack was anticipated by Ewell's Confederates, who advanced from their breastworks at 4:45. The Wilderness again altered tactics. The two sides fought through swamps and marshes to a stalemate. Since they couldn't even see one another, both armies took aim at the sound of firing, hoping it was the enemy they were shooting at. By 8:00 a.m., as the musketry died, the shrieks and groans of the wounded could be plainly heard, spreading the impression to even more men that they may indeed have stumbled into Dante's Inferno.

Nearly two hours late, at about 6:30 a.m., Burnside's Union troops began their march toward the Chewning Farm, between the Orange Turnpike and Orange Plank Road. But then their commander called a halt so his men could have their coffee and breakfast. As they ate, they heard fighting on either side of them. By 7:30 they were under way again, having wasted much precious time.

Whether the delay aided the Confederates or not is debatable, but in battle, any additional time given the enemy to prepare is costly to an attacking force. As they marched onto the battlefield, Confederate artillery began raking them and Confederate infantry blocked their route. Their commander called a halt to the advance when he realized the Rebels occupied the high ground at the Chewning Farm.

Confusion caused by the Wilderness, which had become as much a participant in the battle as either army, dictated the outcome of the next few hours. Union attacks from the north on Longstreet ran out of gas; as well, an attack by a Northern brigade, in the tangled underbrush, blundered blindly into the Confederates and paid dearly for it. In the Wilderness, a coordinated attack seemed impossible to achieve. By 10:00 a.m. Union and Confederate forces ground to a stalemate.

Earlier, scouts reported to Longstreet about an unfinished railroad bed that paralleled the Orange Plank Road. He sent his staff to reconnoiter, then came up with a plan to use the bed as a guide for an attack upon the Union left flank. An hour before noon, Confederates swarmed over the swales of earth between the railroad bed and the Union flank. Coming out of the Wilderness, one Federal thought they looked like ghosts rising from the earth.

Longstreet sent artillery east on the Orange Plank Road, then rode in front of the column of his infantry with his staff and officers.

Confusion, normal for the fighting in the Wilderness, now handed the Rebels a crushing blow. Just crossing the road as Longstreet and his entourage approached was the Rebel column. In the hazy smoke, they mistook the group of officers for the enemy and fired. Confederate Brig. Gen. Micah Jenkins took a heavy, lead minié ball into his brain, through the temple. The handsome twenty-eight-year-old South Carolinian slumped from his horse to the ground, continuing to talk, issuing nonsensical orders, still, in his destroyed brain, fighting the battle. Perhaps worse, Longstreet himself was hit. Though a large, heavy man, the bullet lifted him from his saddle. The projectile hit him in the neck and passed out his right shoulder. Though choking on his own blood, his surgeon managed to staunch the bleeding and save his life. Not so for poor Micah Jenkins.

Burnside, in the meantime, had reorganized his troops to continue his attack. But before the attack could begin, Burnside had to have his lunch. What can only be called a champagne picnic came out for him and his staff. They apparently felt no compunction pausing and consuming the meal while soldiers of other corps died around—and possibly because of—them. Finally, some eight hours after he began to get into position, his attack upon Longstreet's flank stepped off. He was partially successful in drawing some of Longstreet's men to the area; had Hancock advanced out from the breastworks and attacked Longstreet, much may have been gained. But Hancock froze, intimidated, some claimed, by the complete confusion brought on by his few hours fighting in the Wilderness.

Hancock's men had cleared a field of fire and cut down abatis—fallen trees with sharpened branches pointing toward the enemy—and had artillery backup. He must have felt somewhat secure behind the breast-high logs. But at 4:15 p.m., they heard the high tones of bugles echoing through the pines of the Wilderness. Confederates, whooping the Rebel yell, advanced toward them across the clearing. They were stopped by Yankee rifle-muskets, but fell to their knees, refusing to fall back, and fired toe to toe with Union infantry at thirty yards. The brush between them burst into flames. The wind was blowing toward the Federal line. The dry log breastworks caught, and the fire and smoke accomplished what the Rebels could not, driving the Federals from their position. Soon, through the smoke, Confederate battle flags could be seen waving over the earthworks along the Brock Road.

But the part of the Union line the Confederates had captured was directly in front of the Union artillery, which was backing their infantry. No sooner did the Rebels place their flags upon the breastworks than the gunners blew them off. The Federals were using double-canister ammunition (small iron balls packed into a tin can) to fire, shotgun-like, from the cannons at massed infantry. Their artillery bought time for Federal infantry to reorganize. The fighting was hand to hand with men using the bayonet and clubbed muskets. For fifteen minutes it raged until the Yankees won back their breastworks.

The Federal high command had seen that for a breakthrough, all they needed was a coordinated attack. The scheduled attack was for 6:00 p.m., but Longstreet's assault on Hancock at 4:15 had ruined that opportunity. The coordinated assault was called off. But nobody told Burnside. Again the Wilderness, with its dead-end trails and impenetrable line of sight, became a player. The only thing obvious to Burnside's men marching through the woods was the carnage in every conceivable out-of-the-way place. A Michigan commander observed the dead and dying scattered through the woods beside them for a half-mile, and thought it demoralizing to the men about to enter the fray. Once the fighting began, conditions were no better than before. Another Union officer declared that they could not see thirty yards in any direction. Strangely, by nightfall the small trees had been pruned away by musket balls and the visibility was greatly improved. But by then, Burnside's attack had been repulsed.

Confederate general John B. Gordon had spent the day scouting above the Orange Turnpike. He found what he called "temporary" breastworks in the woods, around which lounged Union soldiers, rifles leaning against the works, cooking and boiling coffee. Just in front of the dense woods was a clearing in which he could form his troops for an attack. From this position, he realized that the Union right and rear were exposed to him. It was the type of flank attack that Stonewall Jackson would approve of. He'd seen victory slip from the grasp of the Confederates before, and he was convinced that here was an opportunity rarely presented in war, more impressive even than those missed at Gettysburg.

Unfortunately for the Confederates, when Gordon's proposal for an attack started up the chain of command, it was received with skepticism. Perhaps the confused, nontraditional style of fighting the Wilderness forced upon the combatants had its effect upon the commanders. In later years, as the aging Confederates were wont to do, blame and counter allegations over this, another "turning point" in the war, flew thickly. Suffice it to say, the assault was postponed until half a day after Gordon had discovered the exposed Union flank.

Around 6:00 p.m., the off-guard Union soldiers of the 4th New York Heavy Artillery Regiment were busy gathering up the dead and burying them in a trench. The rest stacked rifles, hung cartridge belts and boxes, and began cooking dinner. Suddenly, out of the dark woods came Southern infantry, screeching their Rebel yell. Ignoring their cooking dinners, the Yankees ran. Gordon's attack dislodged much of the Union line and caught two Union generals in the trap. Darkness and Union reinforcements halted Gordon for good. For the rest of his life he would mourn the mishandling of his proposal for an earlier attack.

The fighting, for the most part, was over. Without a doubt, there were three combatants on May 5–6, 1864: the Union Army, which fought the Confederate Army, and the Wilderness, which fought them both. Rather than calling it a "battle," participants referred to it as a "riot," "bushwhacking," and "Indian fighting." The Wilderness had presented the Union command with difficulties they had never before encountered. Grant and Meade could not use their army's numerical advantage; the Wilderness disallowed the movement of large bodies of troops from one area to another, and so the fighting was done, for the most part, on the brigade level, something the Confederates could handle. The Union artillery's numerical advantage over its Rebel counterpart was negated by the thick woods.

Shakespeare wrote, "Confusion now hath made his masterpiece." Such was the Battle of the Wilderness. Though considered a Confederate victory, there was something different about it, and it had to do with the new Union commander.

Other Federal commanders, after a defeat, withdrew to gather reinforcements and plan another elaborate campaign against the wily Robert E. Lee. At the head of his army, Grant and his staff reached a vital crossroads—one road leading back north, the other south. He turned the head of his horse southward . . . and his soldiers cheered. They sensed that there would be no turning back until the war was over.

Casualty reports differ, but the National Park Service historians have put the figures at about 8,000 killed, wounded, and missing or captured for the Confederates, and some 18,000 casualties lost to the Union. Others sources place the Confederate losses as high as 11,400, and reduce Union casualties to 13,948. The way the Wilderness seemed to consume human beings, we may never know.

In Greek mythology, the River Styx ran between the worlds of the living and the dead. Some of the college-educated officers and men may have looked back, after the next year of fighting, and realized that the River Styx was no mythical place; it was the Rapidan River of Virginia.

If there is any battlefield in America where ghosts linger, it must be the Wilderness. All of the elements paranormalists agree upon are there to create ghosts.

Young men with much left to do in life died violent, sudden, sometimes unexpected deaths. Many of the suffering wounded, already in horrible pain and unable to move, died a horrific death from the creeping flames. Their fellow soldiers, watching from only a few feet away, were unable to help them because of the intense heat. Some of those wounded were seen, as the flames slowly moved closer, to load their weapons and place the muzzles under their chins.

Human emotion produces energy. When a human is struggling desperately to stay alive, there can be no more powerful emotions emanating, except perhaps when that individual is actually dying. When another wants more than ever to rescue a friend from dying, and cannot, human emotion peaks at its highest levels.

One religious tenet associated with producing ghosts is burial in unconsecrated ground.

As with many battlefields of the Civil War, there may still be many soldiers who died on the Wilderness Battlefield buried there. The first burial parties claimed proudly they had found and buried all the bodies; later burial details bemoaned the fact that their predecessors had done such a slipshod job. There may be many soldiers' remains, hastily buried by comrades and forgotten, scattered about the field.

As well, houses may hold the energy of the living long after they are dead, especially if those spirits can return to the site of important or traumatic events in their lives. Often, when those buildings are being renovated or restored, paranormal activity increases.

Ellwood Manor was built around 1790. In its early years, the large, two-story brick house was visited by "Light Horse" Harry Lee (Robert E. Lee's father), the Marquis de Lafayette, James Madison, and James Monroe.

The Lacy family, who also owned Chatham, across the river from Fredericksburg, owned Ellwood and used it as a summer home until the Civil War disrupted their lives. First occupied by Confederates after Chancellorsville, it was used as a recovery hospital. Stonewall Jackson's left arm was amputated in a nearby field hospital. Beverly Tucker Lacy, brother of the owner, was Jackson's chaplain, and brought the arm to the Lacy Family Cemetery, a hundred yards or so from the house, where it was buried and remains today.

In 1864, during the Battle of the Wilderness, the parlor of the house became Union major general Gouverneur K. Warren's headquarters. Grant's headquarters were nearby, and he visited Ellwood to plan the battle with Warren.

Ellwood has been restored to its May, 1864, appearance by generous donations from the Friends of the Wilderness Battlefield, and is now a part of the Fredericksburg and Spotsylvania National Military Park. During its restoration, numerous unexplainable events occurred.

Many years ago, according to locals, a visitor to Ellwood committed suicide by shooting himself in one of the upstairs rooms. More recently, during the restoration of the house, a Fredericksburg man and a friend had driven out after dark and parked to do some ghost hunting. After they passed through a cornfield, they approached the back of the house.

Suddenly they began hearing things coming from the house: First, a loud bang came from inside; then the sound of something being dragged across a wooden floor. After they turned on their flashlight, they heard the bang again. Illuminating one of the lower windows, the man saw shadows rush from left to right across the first-floor window on the left. He followed with the light what would have been the shadow's movement inside, to the right-hand window. Both he and his friend saw the same thing: the figure of a man in his seventies, with a thin, wispy beard and wearing a blue coat.

Frightened at the apparition, he and his friend ran. Once they got in the car he asked his friend what he had seen. Without prompting, he described the same man. It wasn't until then that he began to research the house; he soon learned that the National Park Service had no rangers living there at the time. The house was unoccupied and locked up by the federal government.

A woman who has lived in Spotsylvania County all her life told of once seeing the strange lights that have been seen before, named by locals the "Phantom Fires of the Wilderness." They are seen at night on the western edge of the Wilderness from Route 15, between Culpeper and Orange. When individuals go to examine them, there is never any evidence that fires have burned in the area—no burned wood, still-smoldering coals, or scorched ground. In paranormal circles they are sometimes called "ghost lights" or "spooks' lights," and are common supernatural phenomena. Could observers be seeing through a warp or tear in time into the past, when the campfires of armies, a hundred thousand strong, once bedded down there before marching to their deaths?

The Wilderness of Civil War lore was a wilderness hundreds of years before the war brought it infamy. And today it retains much of its wild character, with the exception of a few islands of private property within it. The modern, well-kept homes sitting where men once roasted to death are not as peaceful as they should be.

A woman told me of seeing strange, human-like shadows crossing her backyard at night. They seem to come out of nowhere and disappear just as mysteriously. Of course, running through her yard are the remains of Civil War era earthworks, where men fought viciously and died tragically. She says it happens so often that her family has become accustomed to seeing the ghostly figures.

Then there is the former federal law enforcement officer, living in a beautiful modern house, whose wife once looked down her hall to see a soldier of the Civil War in a tattered uniform moving across the hallway. She and her husband inspected the spot, found no one in any of the rooms, and so came to the only conclusion possible: It had been a visitor from another era.

I have done paranormal investigations, along with my wife Carol, on the Wilderness Battlefield numerous times. We were investigating near one of the temporary cemeteries indicated on the battlefield, where the dead were buried before being moved to the national cemetery in Fredericksburg. Carol began to use her dowsing rods as she walked along. Each time she came to one of the depressions where a body had been located, the rods crossed, indicating that there may be remnant energy, even in empty graves. When she moved out of the depression, the rods uncrossed.

On July 18, 2005, I picked up some EVP (electronic voice phenomena) near where the Stonewall Brigade, Jackson's first command, fought. I asked a few questions about the unit, including asking their commander's name. I already knew that James A. Walker commanded the brigade during the battle, but I got a voice saying a name that sounded like "Frazer." Later research uncovered the fact that a regiment in the brigade, the 27th Virginia, had just received a new commander on the morning before the battle, a nineteen-year-old who was killed that day by a bullet to the head. His name: Philip Frazer.

19

THE BATTLE OF SPOTSYLVANIA COURT HOUSE

Gettysburg is a skirmish compared to this fight.

—George W. Burchell, a soldier from the Iron Brigade

Former commanders of the North's Army of the Potomac, after being defeated by Lee's Army of Northern Virginia, usually retreated back north across the Potomac, to request more men and reorganize for another "On to Richmond" attempt. But the new commander, Ulysses S. Grant, was different. Instead of retreating after the costly fighting in the Wilderness, he turned southward. It was an indication of the type of war that would be fought from this point forward.

His objective was a crossroads—actually a "T"-shaped junction, with several other roads converging nearby—that would lead his army around the Confederates' right flank. The route would force Lee out of the tangled Wilderness and into the open to fight a battle on a field of Grant's choosing.

Near the "T" was the Spotsylvania County Court House, which would lend its name to some of the most desperate fighting in the entire Civil War.

Because of the actions of Grant's predecessors, Lee was unsure of Grant's intentions, so had to be prepared for any movement his enemy might make. While part of his army remained in place but ready to march, he ordered Richard Anderson—now commanding

Longstreet's Corps after Longstreet had been wounded—to march toward Spotsylvania Court House at 3:30 a.m., May 8.

But the sickening smell of the bodies of men and horses cooking off in the burning woods pushed Anderson to march hours earlier than ordered, and to continue the march, not halting until the last of his men had emerged from the nauseous air. Because of this, Lee had inadvertently gotten a half-day head start on Grant.

Again, the Wilderness, like some unwanted entity, intervened in the deadly pursuits of men: If it wasn't for the fires in the Wilderness, Grant could have blocked Lee from getting to Spotsylvania, and the American Civil War may have ended a year earlier.

Anderson got to the area of Spotsylvania Court House at around 8:30 a.m. on May 8, literally just a few minutes before the Federals. He sent two brigades toward the Spotsylvania Court House "T" to push back any Yankee horsemen headed there, and had two more climb Laurel Hill to hold off the Union foot soldiers of Grant's Fifth Corps, advancing south on the Brock Road. As the vanguard of Anderson's men crested the hill, they were met by none other than the famed Confederate cavalry commander, Maj. Gen. J. E. B. Stuart himself, whom Anderson let take command of his infantry in this sector. "Run for the rail piles," Stuart called out to the troops, to encourage them to sprint to the top of the hill. "The Federal infantry will reach them first if you don't run."

The Southerners got to the "rail piles" first and used them as breastworks, just as the Union troops came advancing across Spindle Field, a clearing to the north of Laurel Hill. Stuart was described by one observer as being as "cool as a piece of ice" and laughing, as always, seemingly joyous with the prospect of battle.

The heat was oppressive for early May, and the Union troops were exhausted from marching all night from their battlefield in the Wilderness. For them, Spindle Field became an open killing zone. Wounded officers tumbled from their mounts. The United States Regulars, professional soldiers in an army of volunteers, took horrendous casualties. One Regular regiment of five hundred finished the battle with only seventy-five men. Those Union troops who did manage to cross Spindle Field engaged in bayonet-to-bayonet fighting with Southerners who held the hill. All the while, Stuart, oblivious to danger, rode among the men along the top of the hill, laughing and joking with them to keep their spirits high. With Union cavalry about to head toward Richmond—and a rendezvous to keep with a Yankee bullet at Yellow Tavern—Stuart had only four days left to live.

Losses in the Federal's Fifth Corps were growing to unsustainable levels. Confederates were flanking them in the open area of Spindle Field. Survivors sought refuge in the rear near their artillery, and blamed their superior officers, who sent them in piecemeal.

Around 11:00 a.m. Confederate gunners placed their cannons just below the crest of Laurel Hill, using its elevation as a natural breastwork, exposing only the muzzles to the enemy. They opened fire on Union troops massing for another try. Eventually all of the Corps artillery—some fifty cannons—were firing. The exploding shells created pandemonium in the packed Union reserves.

Not to be outdone, an equal number of Federal guns were gathered and opened fire. The duel lasted until about 1:00 p.m., but to no military advantage for either side.

During this time a contretemps blew up at Grant's headquarters that had lasting effects on the battle—and the war.

Throughout the battle during the morning, it seemed that famed Union cavalry commander Phil Sheridan and army commander George Meade had been getting in each other's way. When the fiery Sheridan entered the excitable Meade's tent, they had it out. Sheridan felt constrained, having to fight under Meade. Meade thought the cavalry had clogged up the roads, interfering with the passage of his infantry. Grant's tent was nearby, and Meade took his grievance to him, repeating his conversation with Sheridan, including Sheridan's comment that he could whip J. E. B. Stuart if only Meade would get out of his way. That comment caught Grant's attention, since he had served with Sheridan early in the war and knew him well.

"Did Sheridan say that?" Grant inquired. "Well, he generally knows what he is talking about. Let him start right out and do it."

Meade wrote the orders sending Sheridan after Stuart by 1:00 p.m., probably happy to get him out of his hair. With that decision, Grant lost his cavalry for the rest of the battle. But Sheridan was true to his boast: He not only found J. E. B. Stuart, but also his cavalry, mortally wounding him, and thereby removing Stuart, one of the finest cavalry commanders on either side, from the Confederate war effort.

By 1:30 Meade had ordered more Union infantry to assist the Fifth Corps in the advance across Spindle Field and the taking of Laurel Hill. Meade's orders were for an immediate assault, to drive the Rebels from the hill. The troops did not arrive on the Laurel Hill battlefield, however, until early evening, and the combined units were not prepared for an attack until some five hours after Meade had issued the orders. By the time they finally got organized for their assault, they faced a Confederate line that had had all day to dig in, and was reinforced.

As well, a certain strange miasma seemed to overwhelm the Northerners, from commanding general on down. Many of them had gone nights without sleep and then attempted an all-night, hurried march. The weather was described as the most sultry of the spring. Men were hungry and thirsty and footsore. Officers, too, were affected, and showed a carelessness throughout the fighting on May 8.

As they marched past fought-over fields, the curse of the Wilderness never seemed far from haunting them. On one of the roads they passed woods on fire, and within saw the bodies of Rebels and Federals alike, freshly killed and "scorching."

By 3:30 some of the highest-ranking officers in the Union Army, except for Grant, were gathered; one described them as being "worn and troubled . . . jaded and prostrated." As historian Gordon C. Rhea wrote: "Hard marching, sleepless nights, and protracted fighting had 'produced a powerful effect on the nervous system of the whole army.'"

But Meade wanted something to show for the day's fighting. He needed the road to Spotsylvania Court House open, and so, at about 6:30 p.m., launched another assault.

Daylight was waning. In just a few minutes of fighting one Union brigade lost 150 men and was repulsed, accomplishing nothing. Reinforcing Confederates came onto the field, swung to the right of the existing breastworks on Laurel Hill, and launched a charge of their own against the retreating Federals. Darkness made it almost impossible to determine friend from enemy. Though small fights went on through the darkness, both sides were too exhausted to continue any large-scale operations.

The Union advance to Spotsylvania Court House was stymied.

The rest of the Confederate Army arrived on the battlefield and began moving into position on May 9. Their line soon resembled an inverted "V," with a bulging salient at the apex, which began to be called the "Mule Shoe" for its shape. Even the lowliest private gets nervous when he can see the backs of his comrades in the trenches. It means that the position can be enfiladed on either side: Shells and bullets fired at one side of the salient will fall unnervingly in the rear of the other. Soldiers may face fire, but bullets coming from the side or behind are hard to stand. Also, any breakthrough on one side of the bulge will end up in the rear of the other side, another situation soldiers find untenable. The only advantage it offered Lee was an interior line: Troops could be moved quickly across the area behind the lines from an inactive spot in the curved line to an endangered one. (An exterior line means troops must be moved along the outside of a curved line, thus spending more time on the march to an endangered spot.) A correspondent visiting the army at the time wrote that "it was Gettysburg reversed—Lee having the inner circle."

But as the troops engaged were soon to find out, it was worse than Gettysburg. Far worse.

And a hero of Gettysburg would fall. Maj. Gen. John Sedgwick, who commanded the Federal Sixth Corps, had been told of Rebel sharpshooters across from the Spindle Farm, where some of his artillery was stationed. He was out inspecting his lines and was told by an aide that near the artillery several men had been shot by a deadly accurate Rebel sharpshooter. Sedgwick expressed the fact that he didn't think he would need to go there. Later, he saw a problem with the positioning of some of his troops. Intent on his duty as a corps commander, he forgot the warnings and moved to the position.

Moving troops invited the whiz and splat of Confederate bullets, and his troops started to duck the missiles. Typically for Sedgwick, he teased them, telling them he thought the sharpshooter too far away to be of any harm: "They can't hit an elephant at that distance."

Then there was a hollow thud. Sedgwick turned slowly, then fell onto one of his aides, a neat, round bullet hole just below his left eye, the smile from teasing his men still on his face. He was one of the most popular general officers in either army. J. E. B. Stuart, heading off to his own demise, heard about Sedgwick, whom he had known and liked before the war. Even Stuart, his enemy, mourned his death.

Both commanders hoped to use May 9 as a rest, refitting, and entrenching day, and to bring up additional troops, rations, and ammunition. Grant planned and attempted to launch an assault on the Confederate left, but by the time all was ready, darkness forced cancellation of the attack. The main action occurred on the Confederate right flank on the Fredericksburg Road. Union general Ambrose Burnside (defeated at Fredericksburg in 1862) sent part of his Ninth Corps south on the road from Fredericksburg to Spotsylvania Court House. Their march was held up, lending truth to Meade's earlier complaints, by Sheridan's cavalry, beginning their ride toward Richmond. After the road was clear, they continued their march and ran into Confederates at the Ni River. The ensuing battle lasted until afternoon. The result was, once again, to deny the Spotsylvania Court House road junctions to the Federal army.

There was another ominous portent: Any plans of Grant's were now hindered by his lack of cavalry and the information on the enemy they could bring. His hasty, offhand remark about his friend Sheridan left him without eyes and ears.

May 10 was to bring about Union attacks, first on the Confederate left, then on their now well-fortified position on Laurel Hill. Both ended with the attackers being caught in flames when the dry pine needles and scrub brush caught on fire, à la the Wilderness. Grant, by then, had planned an all-out assault on the entire Confederate line, and scheduled it to begin at 5:00 p.m. Grant planned it, but without Sheridan's cavalry, he once again lacked information on the Rebel positions.

On the afternoon of May 10, Union colonel Emory Upton, just twenty-four years old, received his orders to attack the Confederates' position on the west face of the Mule Shoe salient. Upton, for all his youth, was an innovator in tactics.

Tactics in the American Civil War were based upon the same late-eighteenth-century procedures used by Napoleon, the recognized European genius of the battlefield. Most military manuals studied at the US Military Academy at West Point were based upon Napoleonic tactics. Those who studied them from the 1820s through the 1850s would become the officers who fought the Civil War—on both sides.

So the standard for an attack was for soldiers to line up shoulder to shoulder and march—walk—toward the enemy line until they got within sprinting distance, say fifty yards. Then they would fire a volley at the defenders and rush to capture the position with the bayonet.

During Napoleon's time, the weapons used, for the most part, were smooth-bore muskets firing a round ball. Basically a tube, the weapon had a range of not much more than one hundred yards, and an effective range of fifty to seventy-five yards. An attacking line could walk to within that range, receive one volley from the defenders, fire their volley, and sprint the fifty-yard interval between lines to finish the job with the bayonet.

During the 1850s, however, a Captain Minié of the French military designed a conical-shaped projectile with an indentation in the base. When used in a musket with rifling grooves (literally, with a twist inside the barrel), the indentation softened from the heat of exploding powder and expanded to fill the grooves. The result was that the bullet came out spinning. The effective range increased from seventy-five yards to well over three hundred. Attackers could not be expected to sprint three hundred yards and engage defenders in hand-to-hand combat. So they continued to walk in lines, taking several volleys (since a trained soldier in a stationary defensive position could load and fire around three times per minute), as well as tremendous casualties.

Though the tactics Upton was about to use were not new, they were specialized, and could be used only at certain times against certain defensive positions.

First, the position to be attacked had to have a convex curve so that the defenders' fire would spread out rather than concentrate. Second, the attackers must not have to cross too wide a field in order to lessen their exposure in the open. Finally, the defenders' artillery must not be able to fire upon the attackers.

Engineers thought they had found the perfect spot in the Mule Shoe salient. Rather than attacking with lines spread thin along a wide front, Upton would mass his troops in a column. He would punch a hole in the salient. After that, each succeeding unit would have specific assignments to spread out into the salient and attack the defenders.

Upton formed his twelve regiments in a column three regiments wide and four deep, numbering about five thousand men. He was told he would be supported by more Union troops to his left, keeping those enemy soldiers occupied.

There was a grassy road that led directly to the Confederate position and would serve as a guide to Upton's attack. Once in position, the troops were told to remain silent and fix bayonets. Upton issued the order to load, but only the front line was to "cap" their weapons—to allow them to fire. The men were told they were not to cheer during the assault, nor stop to fire at the enemy. They must cross the open area as quickly as possible, and the officers were to give but one command repeatedly: "Forward!"

There was a Federal artillery bombardment. As soon as that ceased, Upton's supporting Federal attack to his left began—prematurely, as it turned out, since Upton's bombardment was still blasting away at the Confederates in his front.

When the bombardment ended, about 6:10 p.m., Upton's column began its assault at the double-quick, with Upton riding just ahead, the only mounted man in the column. They quickly closed upon the Confederate salient. The first men in the column were literally sacrificed to enemy fire; but the column moved inexorably forward until it struck the earthworks of the salient.

Men now fought each other with muskets as clubs and the bayonet. Some soldiers, not wanting to climb the earthworks to expose themselves, threw their bayoneted muskets javelin-style so they arched over the works; others raised their firearms over the earthworks and pulled the trigger, firing blindly into the mass of the enemy below.

The "battering ram" tactics worked . . . for a while. Upton's men pierced the Confederate salient almost to its center, but Southern artillery stopped Upton's supporting troops on the left before his assault even got started, and a counterattack pushed him back to his starting point. But Grant took notice: If a dozen regiments could break the Confederate salient, what could a much larger force do?

Plans were laid for Federal corps to assault the Rebel salient at dawn on May 12. Robert E. Lee, the Confederate commander, inadvertently assisted Union plans.

On the night of May 11, perhaps once again thinking about former enemy commanders he had faced, Lee began to believe that the Union Army was pulling out of its positions and retreating. To counter the move, Lee started his artillery in the salient on the road. Southern commanders in the Mule Shoe were hearing Union soldiers preparing for an assault in the predawn hours. Panicky, they begged for their artillery to return. Lee rescinded his order, and the artillery began the arduous nighttime backtrack. But it was too late.

Nearly twenty thousand Northern troops slammed into the Mule Shoe, killing Confederates, capturing prisoners, and losing their momentum. By 9:30 a.m., a Confederate counterattack restored just about all of the curved salient. Meanwhile, another Federal corps had been committed to the assault. The fighting reached a crescendo of horror unsurpassed in the annals of military history.

Nature added to the agony. It poured rain as the two armies battled each other furiously for twenty straight hours.

Much of the fighting was done across the earthworks from no more than a yard or two apart. Men splattered each other's brains with musket butts, stabbed blindly at one another through the firing gap in the log breastworks, blasted weapons over the parapets at the massed enemy, not even seeing their target, and walked upon the dead and wounded alike until they were trampled into the water-, blood-, and mud-filled trenches beneath their feet. Leaping upon the works, men crazily fired rifles handed to them until they were shot off, only to be replaced by another, oblivious to the risk to their own lives. By an officer who struggled there, it was called the fiercest hand-to-hand fighting of the war. Or any war.

The living piled up dead bodies to lie behind as gruesome shelter from the bullets. One North Carolina regiment began an advance, led by one soldier loading and firing as he advanced, and singing at the top of his lungs the popular Southern tune, "The Bonnie Blue Flag." His song was abruptly ended when a comrade's musket behind him accidentally discharged, driving a bullet into the back of his skull. The adjutant of the 30th North Carolina regiment was seeking shelter so close to the enemy's breastworks that he was yanked by the hair over the works and became a prisoner. During the charge, the Union momentum was such that the men in the front line literally ran themselves onto Rebel bayonets. The Southern boys, as if they were working as the Devil's farmhands, caught them and pitchforked them overhead like bloody blue bales of hay into the ditch behind the breastworks.

A Federal officer's aide watched as an officer waved to get his attention. An artillery shell hissed in and took off the top half of his head as clean as a razor, just above the jaw. When the aide passed the body, the tongue was still moving, as if the officer were trying to convey something of the Other World into which he had just passed.

The color-bearer of the 16th Mississippi leapt the works with his flag twice, was driven back once, and wounded the second time he mounted the works. A third time his luck ran out, a bullet crashing into his head. The earthworks grew slick with rain, mud, and blood. During what brief lulls there were, the Southern defenders lifted dead bodies from their trenches and flung them outside to give themselves more room to fight.

Men squatted in gore, with "mud, blood, and brains mingled [that] would reach up to my waist." They took on the countenances of wildly painted Indians: "[M]y head and face were covered or spotted with the horrid paint," recalled one.

Artillery that the Yankees attempted to bring forward just crushed the dead and wounded alike under its churning wheels. What cannon they did manage to get into position over the gory carpet was successful. Solid shot blasted through the Confederate log- and earthworks at a range of only about 140 feet. But the artillery horses, the locomotion for the guns, were doomed at such close range, and were killed off by Confederate marksmen (a cruel necessity used by both sides). The gunners were next to be shot down, and soon the cannons had to be abandoned, sunk in the mud up to their wheel hubs.

Confederates also used the artillery returned by Lee and fired point-blank into blue-clad soldiers ranked eight to ten deep. Using canister, the packed balls like giant shotgun shells sliced huge gaps in the tight formations, limbs and torsos cartwheeling above a crimson mist. Union troops closed those gaps under fire, but found themselves hindered by piles of dead bodies interfering with their tactical movements.

Federals brought up mortars—cannons which lofted shells high in the air to land behind the Confederate earthworks, since flat-trajectory artillery killed attackers as well as defenders. Their bloody effectiveness became amusement for some of the assaulting soldiers. Apparently bored by the maddening tedium of death that continued hour after hour, some New Jersey troops bet on what body part would be blown over the parapet next: An arm? A leg? A head? One mortar shell exploded near the 16th Mississippi's flag, decapitating a Confederate, whose dying body remained standing upright, blood spurting out of the neck like some bizarre, devilish fountain.

While state-of-the-art artillery was used, so were the most primitive of weapons. When the enemy was so close he couldn't use his musket, one Mississippian grabbed a camp hatchet and split the skull of an oncoming Yankee with it. Other Confederates, realizing a hatchet's utility during close-in fighting, found their own and used them.

At one point in the Confederate breastworks, a twenty-two-inch (in diameter) oak tree tumbled, felled by the steady, random chipping away of small-arms fire. Its location would become a battlefield landmark, with everyone from private soldiers to Lee himself examining it as a horrifying tribute to the effectiveness of small-arms fire in battle. The remnant of the stump would end up in the Smithsonian Institution. An officer from New Jersey wrote that for each new assault and repulse, fresh bodies fell on the already-heaped slain, and across the ditches the living fought on the corpses of those already fallen. Still-living wounded were buried along with the dead, both trampled by those still fighting into the red-tinted mud at the Mule Shoe.

Darkness brought some relief. Decimated Union units withdrew under the cover of night. Still, firing roared on past midnight. By 3:00 a.m., a new Rebel line across the base of the Mule Shoe had been created. Exhausted Confederates still alive in the salient got the order to withdraw to the newly fortified position. It had been constructed with time bought by the lives of those who now would never use it.

Dawn exposed to unbelieving eyes evidence of what was arguably the fiercest, bloodiest conflict of an already fierce, bloody war. Daylight showed limbs protruding from the muck still moving. Soldiers ganged together and pulled other men out of the waist-deep quagmire by their extremities, incredibly still breathing. Wounded were exhumed from beneath hills of the dead, hardly recognizable as human. The corpses were described as lumps of meat or clotted gore, as would be seen in a butcher's shop. The wounded perhaps had a chance to crawl out of the line of fire; the dead were hit time and again, eventually "chopped into hash by the bullets," looking more like "piles of jelly" than anything human. The dead were piled four deep in places. Even close friends could not be recognized. One man found a comrade who didn't have four inches of space on his body that hadn't been hit. His friend counted eleven bullet holes through one of the soles of his shoes. The Confederates retreated and the Federals were left with the salient—and the Confederate bodies, which were thrown into the trenches, once so carefully constructed, and covered over with the excavated mud.

The final tally from May 12 was appalling: Some nine thousand Federals became casualties on that day; the Rebel army lost about eight thousand. Seventeen thousand casualties in twenty hours.

MULE SHOE AND SPOTSYLVANIA COURT HOUSE INVESTIGATIONS

With such unprecedented slaughter, it's no wonder that the area around the Mule Shoe and Spotsylvania Court House is known to be haunted—perhaps by those doomed to die in battle there, and possibly by others as well.

Paranormalists have identified a number of reasons why perturbed spirits of the dead might linger at a certain place on earth: a youthful death; a violent death; unfinished business left on earth; a sudden death, where the spirit doesn't know that the body is dead; and, in some religious circles, an unconsecrated burial. All of these, of course, apply to battlefields everywhere. Certainly they apply specifically to the battlefield of Spotsylvania.

One lifelong resident of the area recalls her mother telling her that she would go down to the courthouse and battlefields at night over the anniversary of the battle and see long columns of ghostly infantry marching in the distance. Her grandfather also talked of seeing the dead walking; he observed slaves strolling around his house and in the fields, nearly a century after all the slaves had been freed.

The Mule Shoe has also been called "The Bloody Angle," and has had its share of paranormal activity, some of which can be documented by modern methods.

In 2005, experiments with EVP (electronic voice phenomena) at the Bloody Angle near the marker for the fallen oak tree yielded results. Although burial parties scoured the area in 1866–1868 and brought to cemeteries hundreds of bodies, it is well known that in operations like this, many more bodies are missed and remain buried where they fell. It can only be assumed that such was the case at the Bloody Angle, particularly since the fighting took place in the pouring rain, where the trenches filled waist-deep in water and mud, and where the dead and wounded were often buried by trampling feet where they died. Many may still remain buried there.

My protocol for attempting to gather EVP is to set my Panasonic digital recorder on "voice activation" to record only when the machine picks up sound. I will ask a question pertinent to the people or place where I'm recording. Then I wait thirty to forty-five seconds in silence. Often, the recorder will begin to record during that time. The unnerving part is that you cannot hear anything while the machine is recording, but that's the nature of EVP: It is *electronic* voice phenomena, and the human ear cannot hear electromagnetic waves, only sound waves propagated through a medium like air.

At the Bloody Angle while attempting to record EVP, my wife Carol and I both heard a crashing noise in the far tree line. She thought it sounded like a tree falling, but we heard no chain saw. I knew exactly what it sounded like, because I had heard it so many times before at reenactments: Definitely, without a doubt in my mind, it was what was called in Civil War Era literature, the "rattle of musketry," echoing, unexplainable, across the great, flowing mystery of time.

Interestingly, though two people heard it, the recorder did not pick it up.

During a second attempt at obtaining EVP, I stood near the monument to men from Ohio who had fought at Spotsylvania. I addressed the men from Ohio as "Buckeyes"—the state tree, and what Ohioans sometimes call themselves. After the first query, "You fought here didn't you?," at five seconds I heard a muffled answer in the affirmative. A second time addressing them, after I said I was proud of them, nine seconds into the recording, I heard a soft, "Thank you, sir."

A later investigation took us to the Spotsylvania Old Jail, which is near the famous, coveted "T" junction, and was used to house some Union prisoners from the battle. As well, it was in the Spotsylvania Court House jail (but not this building) where the Revolutionary War hero "Light Horse" Harry Lee was incarcerated for a while during his imprisonment for indebtedness. In one of those ironies of history, his son, Robert E. Lee, would command the Confederate Army of Northern Virginia in battle near the jail site.

When we walked into the old, but restored, whitewashed jail, in my mind's eye I could see the disarmed, dirty, exhausted, captured boys in blue filing into the little jail and collapsing along the walls, first come, first served, for a seat on the floor.

On our subsequent investigation we had brought some people interested in knowing more about paranormal investigating. We supplied some of them with electromagnetic field (EMF) meters to detect anomalies in the environment. (Keep in mind, no matter what you see on TV, there is *no* such instrument as a "ghost detector." Investigators use sensitive electronic instruments to detect the anomalies that have historically been associated with ghosts: cold spots indicating something absorbing heat energy, or hair on the arms or back of the neck rising, revealing static or electromagnetic energy present. Once detected, the anomalies may be photographed or recorded as EVP.)

One of the women in the jail cell to the left (there were only two cells in the small jail) began following an electromagnetic field where we had never found one before—along the entire wall, but only about waist-high—about the height of the head of a man sitting down, leaning against the wall. She also found an EMF anomaly on the one-foot-thick windowsill that was in motion, continuing to move back and forth.

In an attempt to debunk the results, we checked for electrical wires but there were none. In addition, we knew that several previous investigations yielded no anomalies like the one we were seeing; the effect was temporary, a phenomenon frequently associated with spirit energy, which comes and goes unexplainably. A check outside for underground wiring showed only overhead wires, too high from the building to affect the EMF meters when tested.

Spotsylvania County Court House itself is not the original building that was there at the time of the battle, but some elements of the old courthouse—in particular, the distinctive white columns in front—were incorporated in the new building. The fact that it is not the original apparently doesn't deter the ghosts from enjoying their visit to the courthouse building.

In the offices where the circuit court clerk works, random cold spots are reported by current county employees. Some people, employees and visitors alike, have reported feeling that chill or cold spot, then suddenly, a nearby door will open or close. Also present is the smell of cigar smoke wafting through the offices, even though the facility is smoke-free.

County police officers often come into the courthouse after hours to complete paperwork. While concentrating on their work, they suddenly have their attention drawn to the door, where they will see someone pass by. To be on the safe side, they always investigate, even though they know a search of the building will yield no human walking the halls, since they always lock the doors behind them when they enter the courthouse at night.

There is an underground hallway, sometimes referred to as a tunnel, which connects the newer courthouse with the old. Through it are transported prisoners from cells to the courtrooms for trial. According to officers and employees who travel the underground passageway, it is an extremely haunted site.

And there seems to be video evidence. In the courthouse cellar where prisoners are brought into the courtroom from the underground hallway they are monitored by TV cameras. Witnesses have seen a deputy drop off a prisoner and walk back through the hallway. Officers watching the monitors see individuals following the deputy in the hallway until he reaches the door to the observation room. The door opens and he steps through alone.

Asked who was behind him in the hallway, the befuddled deputy will answer that no one was behind him, having delivered the prisoner and then returned through the subterranean hall alone.

20

A CURSE ON
THE VALLEY

*The people should be informed that so long as an army can subsist among them
recurrences of these raids must be expected, and we are determined to stop them at
all hazards. . . . Give the enemy no rest . . . Do all the damage to railroads and
crops you can. Carry off stock of all descriptions, and Negroes, so as to prevent
further planting. If the war is to last another year, we want the Shenandoah Valley
to remain a barren waste.*

–Ulysses Grant

There is controversy as to the meaning of the name *Shenandoah*,
although the most popular (and appealing) definition of the
Native American word is "daughter of the stars." Standing upon one
of the overlooks just a few yards from the famed Appalachian Trail
and gazing out over the magnificent Valley, it is easy to believe that
somehow this piece of earth was conceived in another world and lent
to humans to solicit their awe.

For generations the lush Shenandoah Valley provided the people
of Virginia with food. When the "War of Northern Aggression" (as
it has been called in the South) came in 1861, the Valley was then
known as the "Granary of the Confederacy," supplier of foodstuffs to
the armies of the Rebellion.

Then during the Civil War it became a battleground, and the
"daughter of the stars" was stained with human blood and tears. As
well as providing the Confederates with provender, it was also a
natural pathway from the South into the North, slicing in a north-

easterly direction through Maryland and into what could have been dubbed the "granary of the North," Pennsylvania. A Confederate army invading from the South merely had to plug up the "gaps" in the easternmost mountain wall of the Blue Ridge and it could move virtually without detection deep into Pennsylvania, a feat which was accomplished several times during the war.

As well, the tricky terrain of the Valley includes Massanutten Mountain, at an altitude of nearly three thousand feet and running for fifty miles, splitting almost a third of the Valley into two sections, with only one road, from Luray to New Market, crossing it. The Shenandoah River, which split into north and south forks, also relegated movements of armies to easily defendable shallow fords and bridges. It was a complicated battleground, to say the least.

But beginning in the spring of 1862, Thomas J. "Stonewall" Jackson laid aside his nom de guerre, indicating a sedentary defensive attitude, and marched his men through the Valley for more than six hundred miles, in a little over a month and a half. They marched so far and so fast that Jackson's troops gained yet another nickname: "Jackson's Foot Cavalry," meaning, they traveled as far and as fast marching on foot as a cavalry force could on horseback.

Their goal that spring was to tie up Union troops in the Valley so that they could not attack the Confederate capital of Richmond from the west, while another Union Army under Maj. Gen. George B. McClellan advanced up the Virginia Peninsula to attack Richmond from the east. Jackson did just that, from March until June, fighting several pitched battles against three different Federal armies and commanders, numbering over 50,000 soldiers. Jackson's force never exceeded 17,000. Jackson's Valley Campaign is considered a classic in military studies, incorporating rapid movement of a small, flexible force to strike and defeat concentrations of the enemy before they can be reinforced. Although always outnumbered, he used interior lines, an intimate knowledge of the Valley terrain, and kept his next moves (much to the dismay of his subordinates, who never knew where they were going next) completely to himself.

The next time the Shenandoah Valley became a battleground was in June, 1863, during what would come to be called the Gettysburg Campaign. After the Confederate victory at Chancellorsville, Gen. Robert E. Lee led his Army of Northern Virginia west from the Fredericksburg area to the Shenandoah Valley, and used it as a natural pathway into the North, plugging the gaps in the mountains with small fighting forces to hide his intentions, and moving into Pennsylvania. In fact, one of the specific goals in invading the North was to draw the war away from the Valley for the summer growing season, to allow them respite from feeding two armies off their land. After the defeat at Gettysburg, Lee's wounded army used the Valley again for their retreat.

By the spring of 1864, the Northern command ordered Gen. Franz Sigel to advance up the Valley to take it out of play for the Confederates. (Contemporary accounts talk about going "up" the Valley when traveling southward, referring to the high altitude at that end of the Valley; conversely, going northward, the armies were said to travel "down" the Valley.) On May 15, 1864, Sigel was defeated at New Market by a Confederate army bolstered by a contingent of 257 young cadets, reluctantly called to duty from the Virginia Military Institute in Lexington. After a grueling two-day march and an assault over a muddy quagmire, they overran some Union artillery and fought their way into the annals of Virginia military legend.

A second Union army under Gen. David Hunter continued the advance southward up the Valley, reaching Lexington, where, in June, they torched the Virginia Military Institute and the house of former Virginia governor Letcher, just for spite. Hunter was stymied in his further efforts by feisty Confederate general Jubal Early, helped by Southern partisans nipping at Hunter's supply lines.

Early cleared the way for his advance down the Valley to the northeast, from which he launched an attack on Washington. Though stopped short of shelling the Northern capital, Early's battle at Monocacy, Maryland, and his attack on Fort Stevens—where Abraham Lincoln became the first (and so far, the last) American president to come under enemy fire—the Confederates proved again how valuable a military resource control of the Valley was.

Responding to Early's bold use of the Valley, the Union high command sent the fiery cavalry commander Philip Sheridan into the area to control the Valley for the North, once and for all.

Politics played into Sheridan's strategy. Lincoln was up for reelection, and Confederates had just shelled and burned Chambersburg, Pennsylvania, a large Northern city. He certainly did not want to add to the arguments of the Peace Party in the North by handing Lincoln another embarrassment. But Lincoln was of another sentiment: He had seen Grant's request to put Sheridan in charge of the campaign in the Valley, and heartily concurred with Grant's orders to Sheridan, to "put himself south of the enemy, and follow him to the death."

Sheridan's philosophy of war certainly matched Lincoln's and Grant's, at least at this stage. Earlier in the summer accusations against Union war-making upon civilian targets such as churches and homes were made in the Richmond newspapers. Sheridan wrote, "I do not believe war to be simply that lines should engage each other in battle and therefore do not regret the system of living on the enemy's country." He went on to say (cynically) that civilians didn't care how many soldiers were killed or wounded as long as they weren't affected. But as soon as the civilians experienced loss of property, the war couldn't end soon enough. He saw that war should become a punishment, and if, "by reducing its advocates to poverty, end it quicker, we are on the side of humanity."

It has a perverse sort of logic, but is all-encompassing: Soldiers are easy to identify; civilians who actually aid the war effort are always hard to pick out; and innocents are harmed just like the guilty. Warfare 150 years ago in the Shenandoah Valley with Sheridan began to have a frighteningly modern ring to it.

Grant wrote to Gen. Henry Halleck in Washington about his intentions concerning the Valley: "If the enemy has left Maryland, as I suppose he has, he should have upon his heels veterans, militiamen, men on horseback, and everything that can be got to follow to eat out Virginia clear and clean as far as they go, so that crows flying over it for the balance of this season will have to carry their provender with them."

So along with the numerous battles Sheridan would fight against armed Confederate soldiers, his men also began what civilian inhabitants of the Valley called, with emphatic understatement, simply "The Burning."

While in the Valley, Sheridan became involved in what would be called, in later days, "cloak and dagger" intrigue. A young Quaker schoolmarm named Rebecca Wright, in spite of living in Winchester, remained loyal to the Union. Because her sister Hannah was a staunch Confederate, she trod on dangerous ground, especially when Thomas Laws, a black vegetable peddler, approached her after having visited the Union lines with his wares. From his mouth he drew a tinfoil pellet which he was to swallow if he had been caught by Confederates. Wrapped inside was a note from none other than the Federal commander in the Valley, Philip Sheridan himself. He told her he was convinced by a subordinate of her loyalty, asked if she could obtain information about the Confederate forces in Winchester, and assured her of the trustworthiness of the bearer.

The night before, a recovering Confederate officer had visited her home, and in casual conversation mentioned that an entire Rebel division with artillery had left Winchester for Richmond. When Laws, the bearer, returned to Sheridan, the general knew that now was the time to attack.

Sheridan pounced on Early in what became known as the third Battle of Winchester, September 19, 1864. (Winchester itself was said to have changed hands between Union and Confederate occupation more than seventy times.) Sheridan, commanding both cavalry and infantry, forced Early's men back to Fisher's Hill. Arriving in Winchester, Sheridan visited Rebecca Wright, met her with jubilation, and wrote his victory telegram to Grant from her home. Two days later, Sheridan beat Early again at Fisher's Hill, then began a slow withdrawal northward back down the Valley, conducting what, in later wars, would be called a "scorched earth" policy of burning barns, mills, homes, and crops, and stealing or killing livestock. Widespread looting—or "foraging," as Sheridan liked to call it—became commonplace.

Things began to get nasty in the Valley because of what came to be called "Partisan Rangers"—the 43rd Virginia Cavalry Battalion, commanded by Lt. Col. John S. Mosby—and the Union cavalry's reaction to them. Mosby's men in modern times would be called guerrilla fighters, local civilians who band together during military emergencies and strike at the organized forces of the enemy. Mosby's men, for the most part, would reside in their homes until word was passed secretly that they were to attack the enemy. They would then don their uniforms, mount up, and gather to strike. After the quick hit, they would virtually disappear again. They became such a thorn in the side of the Union cavalry (who, of course, were burning private barns and mills, destroying civilian farmers' crops in the fields, and stealing personal livestock used for food and to work the fields), that Grant authorized Sheridan to "hang without trial" any of Mosby's men he captured. It was an ill-advised order.

The problem was that Robert E. Lee, J. E. B. ("Jeb") Stuart, Confederate president Jefferson Davis, and the government of the Confederacy recognized the 43rd Virginia Battalion as a legitimate military unit. Grant and the Federal government did not. Things came to a head on September 23, 1864, when some of Mosby's men, numbering just over one hundred, attacked a Federal wagon train approaching Front Royal, in the Valley. They underestimated the military escort for the train and were routed in a quick fight, which cost a lieutenant in the 2nd US Cavalry his life. Lt. Charles McMaster's horse bolted into Confederate lines. Later rumor had Mosby's men shooting him in the head after he had surrendered, an obvious breach in military protocol of the time. During the fighting six of Mosby's men had been captured.

Federal general George Armstrong Custer's men brought them into the town of Front Royal. The town, according to one of the Union cavalrymen, "was in an uproar." Several Union commanders were present, and one, true to Grant's directive, ordered the Confederates executed. Two of Mosby's men were dragged behind the Methodist

Church in town and shot in cold blood. Another was taken to a local farm, stood up against an elm tree, and also shot.

The worst was yet to come. A seventeen-year-old Mosby's Rangers wannabe, Henry C. Rhodes, riding on a borrowed horse, was caught in the roundup. His mother, a widow, ran to the Federals and begged for her boy's life, since he was a civilian. A Union cavalryman threatened to decapitate both of them with his saber. One of Custer's men—with Henry nearly in a faint, and his mother following, pleading for her son—took the young man to a nearby field, stood him up, and fired point blank into him, with all the rounds in his revolver.

The last two prisoners were questioned about Mosby, but refused to talk even after they were offered their lives in return for the information. They were also executed. A sign was quickly drawn up and hung on one of them: "Such is the fate of all of Mosby's men." The sight of their neighbors murdered left a bitterness in the town that lasted far beyond a generation.

When Mosby, who was recovering from a wound, learned of the vicious executions, he put the blame on Custer, who, even then, was known to be hotheaded and impetuous. Mosby sought authorization for retribution through higher channels, stating that he proposed to hang an equal number of Custer's men when captured. General Lee concurred with Mosby's plan, as did the Confederate secretary of war. The Federals' threat of immediate death to Mosby's men did nothing to end his hit-and-run tactics on their army in the Valley.

Mosby later captured some of Custer's men and subjected them to the agony of choosing lots to see which would be executed for the depredations at Front Royal. Some of the captives escaped, but three were hanged near Berryville. Mosby sent a note to Sheridan: "Hereafter any prisoner falling into my hands will be treated with the kindness due their condition, unless some new act of barbarity shall compel me reluctantly to adopt a course of policy repulsive to humanity." Evidently, Custer and the others got the message. Executing Mosby's men wouldn't work in stopping him. Though Sheridan continued to send his cavalry after Mosby's Rangers when they struck, he resumed "The Burning," without Mosby being able to stop it. Still, the band of partisans continued to harass the Yankees in what came to be called, as if it were a separate country, "Mosby's Confederacy," until they were disbanded a dozen days after Appomattox.

Early, hearing that part of Sheridan's force was recalled to reinforce Grant at Petersburg, wigwagged a message so that Union signalmen could intercept it. It purported to be from Confederate general James Longstreet, indicating that his forces were about to join Early and crush Sheridan. Actually, it was a fake message, a gamble to intimidate Sheridan into retreating from the Valley before a vastly superior Rebel force arrived. Sheridan saw through it and didn't take the bait. Making his lines safe, the Union general felt they were secure enough for him to leave for a war conference in Washington.

Cutting his conference with Secretary of War Stanton and General Halleck short, he returned to Winchester, where he stopped for the night of October 18. He received word that all was quiet at his lines at Cedar Creek, about twelve miles to the south of Winchester, and went to sleep.

Early the next morning he was awakened by an officer concerned about the sounds of battle coming from the south. At first Sheridan wasn't worried, but he got up, dressed, and had his horse "Rienzi" saddled while he had breakfast. The distant firing, however, continued.

About 9:00 a.m. Sheridan and his party began their ride toward his lines. As they rode, the sounds of firing ominously grew louder and more continuous. Sheridan even dismounted and put his ear to the ground to discover the sound actually growing closer. They reached a rise in the terrain and Sheridan saw what he most feared: scores of wounded soldiers streaming back toward him; worse, hundreds of unwounded but panicked men, wagons and horses urged on by frightened teamsters, all rushing to get to the rear, a defeated and demoralized army.

Taken by surprise by Early's attack, Sheridan's army had been whipped and had begun a retreat, which turned into the rout Sheridan saw before him. His first thought was to rally them closer to Winchester. While it may have been the militarily prudent thing to do, it was not in Sheridan's character. Instead, he spurred Rienzi forward, riding to the sound of the guns.

Against the flow of his own retreating masses and the enemy somewhere behind them, he rode with just twenty troopers and an aide, carrying his distinctive personal cavalry flag. Waving his cap at the retreating groups of men and shouting to them, "Come on back, boys! Give them hell. Face the other way! We're going to lick those fellows out of their boots! We'll make coffee out of Cedar Creek tonight!"

Somewhere in the confused, disintegrating mass, a couple of soldiers looked at each other, shrugged, and turned back to follow Sheridan; then, a couple more. Some continued to retreat, but most of them turned, drawn by some strange magnetism, and followed Sheridan. A youthful staff officer saw his swallow-tailed guidon and began passing the word to the men that Sheridan had returned to lead them; the young man was future president William McKinley.

As Sheridan got closer to the battlefield he saw some units still fighting, holding their own despite the dissolving army around them. Sheridan called out again, "Men, by God, we'll whip them yet!" The men raised a yell and rallied behind the diminutive figure on the large horse. He found a knot of officers and dismounted. One of the colonels was Rutherford B. Hayes, another future US president. One of the officers told him that they were preparing the best they could for the retreat. "Retreat, hell!" said Sheridan, and told them they'd be back in their old camp by nightfall.

The Confederates, borrowing a page from Lee and Jackson, had earlier stolen around the Union flank and crossed the Shenandoah River, attacking just before dawn. The Union left rolled up like a rug and men skedaddled for their lives. By 10:30 a.m., though, their attack had lost steam. Early summed it up after the war: "The Yankees got whipped and we got scared."

Their slowdown coincided with Sheridan's arrival. He reorganized his officers and men, calling into line additional Federal troops and rallying them to those who still stood. Finally he rode the lines himself, waving his cap to the cheers echoing through the Valley.

Early's delay in pressing his attack was fatal. Custer's men were sent forward to flank the Confederates on their left. With their flank disintegrating, the center soon followed, and they retreated over Cedar Creek. Belle Grove mansion became the celebratory point for Union officers after the exhilarating day.

Word of Sheridan's feat of rallying a disheartened and routed army spread rapidly, throughout the upper echelon and up to the politicos of Washington. Grant praised him, and Lincoln offered him a major general's rank in the regular army, meaning he'd have a high-ranking position even after the war was over and the volunteers returned home. A poem was written about "Sheridan's Ride," and schoolchildren for years after the war recited it for their classmates, searing the feat into the memory of several generations and turning the little general and his horse into legend.

Sheridan moved on that winter to help Grant in the final spring assaults to crush the Confederacy around Petersburg.

Although "The Burning" brought suffering to the civilians of the Valley, and the memory of the horrors of hangings and shootings of suspected guerrillas lingered, thanks to Mosby, the Shenandoah Valley remained, in the words of one Pennsylvania cavalryman, "the most dangerous place to picket I ever saw."

21

THE CURSE OF
JUDSON KILPATRICK
AND THE
DAHLGREN RAID

It was nearing 5:00 p.m. on July 3, 1863, at Gettysburg. Brig. Gen. Judson Kilpatrick and one of his brigade leaders, Brig. Gen. Elon J. Farnsworth, were overlooking the southern end of the battlefield. In the distance was Big Round Top, Little Round Top, a couple of farmhouses lying in a rock- and tree-strewn valley, and Confederates. Many Confederates. Suddenly, down the ridge gallops a rider at full speed, shouting, "We turned the charge; nine acres of prisoners!"

The charge he was so excited about was Pickett's Charge, the climax of the infantry battle at Gettysburg. Kilpatrick had his orders to press the enemy, threaten him, and strike at an opportune moment. This, he believed, was it. He turned to young Farnsworth, just four days a brigadier, and ordered him to take his cavalry and charge.

Farnsworth was incredulous. "General," he said, "do you mean it? Shall I throw my handful of men over rough ground, through timber, against a brigade of infantry? The First Vermont has already been fought half to pieces; these are too good men to kill."

"Do you refuse to obey my orders?" Kilpatrick said. Then he added an unwarranted challenge, abhorrent to any soldier: "If you are afraid to lead this charge, I will lead it."

Farnsworth stood in his stirrups. "Take that back!" More words were exchanged, no doubt referencing personal courage. Kilpatrick finally withdrew. "I did not mean it; forget it." It was too late. Farnsworth said, "General, if you order the charge, I will lead it, but you must take the responsibility."

Another exchange between the two was unheard by witnesses, but Farnsworth rode away saying, "I will obey your order." Kilpatrick replied curtly, "I will take the responsibility." If Farnsworth knew anything about his commander, he knew this was probably a lie.

Farnsworth and his three hundred men made the charge over ground totally unsuitable for cavalry action. They ended up riding in a huge circle behind Confederate lines. An Alabama regiment turned around and poured fire into them. Farnsworth had his horse shot out from under him, borrowed a mount from an enlisted man, and doubled back. He was seen waving his saber and charging.

Of the three hundred cavalrymen who started the charge, sixty-five never made it back. One of those was twenty-four-year-old Brig. Gen. Farnsworth. Surgeons later counted five bullet wounds in his body, all of them deemed mortal. Earlier in the war his men had given Judson Kilpatrick the sobriquet "Kill-Cavalry" Kilpatrick. Ordering Farnsworth to charge solidified that moniker. In his official report of the action, Kilpatrick was effusive in his praise of the dead young man, lauding the courage he so recently disparaged to his face. In an effort to defer the responsibility he had vowed to take, he blamed the Union infantry on his right for not attacking after him, which, in his opinion, would have developed into a total rout of the Confederates. Perhaps he was feeling guilty?

It wasn't the only thing Kilpatrick had to feel guilty about during the Civil War.

According to one historian, early on, when the war had just broken out and officers were recruiting men to volunteer for their units, Kilpatrick was sent by his commanding officer in the 5th New York Infantry to gather infantry recruits for the regiment. He began to work for the competition, talking the men into joining a cavalry unit, of which he was promised the colonelcy. Much to the dismay of his infantry boss, the scam worked. Kilpatrick recruited many as horse-men, and rose to lieutenant colonel in the 2nd New York Cavalry.

While his men trained and lived in a camp outside of Wash-ington, Kilpatrick housed himself in the luxurious Willard's Hotel in town. To help pay for his expensive room, he worked out a "deal" with army suppliers. One testified that he paid Kilpatrick twenty dollars in gold for influencing someone to send a contract his way. Later he would sell horses stolen from Southerners to interests in the North and tobacco to army suppliers, receiving kickbacks.

For one such illegal operation, he was finally confined to the Old Capitol Prison in Washington. But the army needed cavalry leaders, so he was released after serving three months.

Though frequently his military decisions were unsound, his after-action reports made it sound like he was single-handedly win-ning the war. But some of his personal actions belied his reports. Even Robert E. Lee contested exaggerations that ended up in the newspapers about Kilpatrick's cavalry successes during the retreat from Gettysburg, in official dispatches.

In the army of the 1860s, long periods away from loved ones fostered infidelity. Even in such an atmosphere, Kilpatrick's morals—or rather, lack thereof—attracted attention. Judson Kilpatrick had married right out of West Point. After the Gettysburg Campaign in July of 1863, he visited his wife and newborn son. When he returned to duty on August 5, 1863, there was a young woman named Annie Jones who was visiting his headquarters. She soon became his mis-tress, and his men, with tongues in cheeks, referred to her as "General Kill's aide." He procured for her a horse, an officer's jacket and cap, and a pass to go about their camp. It lasted only a couple of weeks before, rumor had it, she moved in with another young cavalry commander, George Armstrong Custer. One historian writes that Kilpatrick had her arrested as a spy and sent to his old stomping grounds, Old Capi-tol Prison. There must have been some truth to the spy rumors, since Union general Meade had the matter investigated.

Other rumors of Kilpatrick's licentiousness swirled among his men, like, why did the general need two black laundrywomen?

On October 19, 1863, Kilpatrick let himself be lured into a trap set by Confederate cavalry commander J. E. B. Stuart, between Buckland Mills and Warrenton, Virginia. The result was the Union cavalry being routed and driven, steeplechase-style, some five miles back to the Mills. It was touted as "The Buckland Races," with Stuart even writing poetry about it.

Kilpatrick suffered personal loss when his wife died in November of 1863. The following January, their infant son died. "Kill-Cavalry" threw himself into his work as only he could: by coming up with a harebrained scheme that would restore him to his pre-Gettysburg glory.

He, like virtually everyone else in the North, had heard of the worsening conditions for Union Army prisoners kept in the hellholes of Libby and Belle Isle in Richmond. Negotiations to restart prisoner exchanges of the early war days had broken down, and overcrowding was causing serious problems. Up to fifteen hundred prisoners per month were dying. Union general Benjamin Butler saw his February raid to free the prisoners turned back by Confederates. Kilpatrick heard of it, and thought he could do it successfully.

Apparently, President Lincoln heard about Kilpatrick's interest and invited him to the White House to discuss it. Lincoln listened to the plan, approved the first two parts of it—freeing the prisoners, and disrupting Confederate communications—and added a third. He wanted proclamations distributed promising amnesty to Rebels who would return to the Union. Kilpatrick left the president for Secretary of War Edwin Stanton's office to work out the details of the three-pronged effort.

Word traveled down the military chain of command. Meade was concerned; Maj. Gen. Alfred Pleasanton, chief of the cavalry branch, wanted nothing to do with it. Meade made it known that the scheme was Kilpatrick's, the president's, and the secretary of war's.

As the plot was being hatched, a young, well-connected amputee showed up at Kilpatrick's headquarters. Col. Ulric Dahlgren, twenty-one-year-old son of navy admiral John Dahlgren, hobbled in on his crutch, having lost his right leg in the fighting after the Battle of Gettysburg. Despite his limited command experience, youthfulness, and wooden leg, Kilpatrick brought the officer in on the scheme, which, with Dahlgren's connections, isn't surprising. Lincoln himself had visited the young man when he was recuperating from his amputation. What is surprising is that Kilpatrick assigned him the main mission of actually raiding the Richmond prisons and releasing the prisoners, the raison d'être of the plan.

On February 28, 1864, Kilpatrick and Dahlgren began their raid, with close to four thousand cavalrymen heading south from the Stevensburg area of Virginia. The plan was for them to eventually split up, with Kilpatrick attacking Richmond from the north, drawing the defenders' attention in that direction. Meanwhile, Dahlgren would take some five hundred troopers and cross the James upriver from Richmond, make their way past the little-defended southern and western approaches, and free the prisoners in Libby and Belle Isle prisons.

One problem it seems no one thought about: How would they transport thousands (one historian estimated eight thousand at Belle Isle alone) of half-starved, ill, weakened men along miles of Southern roads, infested with roaming home guards, all the way down to the end of the Virginia Peninsula, to Fort Monroe? There's no evidence that they brought that many extra horses or wagons, so the malnourished, sickly, unarmed ex-prisoners would apparently have to walk all the way, slowing everyone, including the cavalry, down to a crawl, making them all prime targets for Confederate cavalry and infantry to catch up with them.

Another problem cropped up: After dark on February 29, a storm of heavy rain mixed with snow and sleet blew in on the column, virtually blinding them. At midnight, after twenty-four hours on the march, Dahlgren called a halt for a rest. Very early in the morning of March 1, through the rain and sleet, they saddled up and rode again. They were still about twenty miles from Richmond.

Dahlgren stopped for a while (apparently long enough for a glass of wine) at the home of Confederate secretary of war, James A. Seddon. Mr. Secretary was not home, but his wife was, and after asking for the name of the soaked young officer on a crutch at her doorstep, she said, "I knew you as a boy." She had gone to school with his mother; his father had courted her. She was cordial to the old family friend, and discussed his parents and old times while she sent a servant out the back door to warn Richmond.

Again on the march, around 11:00 a.m., Dahlgren had located the guide supplied by the Federal Bureau of Military Information, the intelligence arm of the government, and was led by him to the crossing point on the James. Because of the horrible weather, the river had swollen and was impassable. Obviously not the fault of the African-American ex-slave, now a bricklayer, who had been supplied by his own government, Dahlgren nevertheless thought he had been betrayed, and executed him by hanging from a nearby tree. Locals left the body swaying for a week as evidence of how the Yankees treat blacks.

In the meantime, Kilpatrick had arrived on the Brook Pike at the northern environs of Richmond and saw no sign of Dahlgren. A dispatch from the younger officer to Kilpatrick had been captured by Rebels. Expecting to charge into Richmond, Kilpatrick's tired men grew anxious. He hesitated and pushed forward skirmishers—dismounted cavalrymen—to discover where the Confederates were. By 1:00 p.m. the full column began their advance, but they ran into heavy resistance which had rallied while Kilpatrick delayed.

As the men began their advance, they got word to halt. Their orders had changed. They were now to begin covering the rear of the column as they retreated. According to one historian, Kilpatrick simply lost his nerve. With that, he abandoned young Dahlgren and began his own withdrawal toward Fort Monroe. Out of danger, he halted and had his men rest.

Dahlgren, meanwhile, weighing his options five miles outside of the Confederate capital, decided to attack. They drove the defending Rebels from their trenches. They were within the city limits and could see the gaslights burning in the streets, but it was as far as they could go. With his already-small force, the losses sustained made him realize that punching his way through to the prisons was now an impossibility. As it was, he had to leave his wounded. With the snow and sleet being driven by the wind, they began their retreat to the northwest.

It was a fighting retreat for both Dahlgren and Kilpatrick.

By now Kilpatrick realized that his magnificent plan, augmented and approved by none other than the president himself, was turning into an ignominious catastrophe. He hardly got near Richmond, he released no prisoners, he cut very few communications, and he lost an admiral's son and personal friend of the president.

He was determined to save something of this unmitigated failure: He would attack Richmond from the east. He woke his men from their death-like sleep. Little did they know as they started their campfires that they were illuminating their position for Confederate cavalry commander Wade Hampton's troopers, who had been following them, waiting for just this moment. The Rebels opened fire and charged. Though inferior in numbers, in the dark, stormy night they gave the impression of a larger force, and routed Kilpatrick, chasing them throughout the rest of the night. Kilpatrick abandoned his crack-brained plan to attack Richmond from the east.

Kilpatrick finally got within Union lines, but only after General Butler had sent out some 3,800 men to his rescue. Still, after failing utterly in his mission, he managed to write a message to General Pleasonton, claiming to have destroyed enemy communications, mills, the canal on the James, and some of the railroad. Northern papers, taking their cue from Kilpatrick, touted his "accomplishments." Southern newspapers said that all he did was add 250 prisoners to the ones he was supposed to liberate. In his official report, he blamed others for his failures: "If Colonel Dahlgren had not failed in crossing the river," or if Butler had attacked from the east—something never included in the original plan—his mission would have been a success.

Dahlgren, meanwhile, had misplaced three-quarters of his command. He was with one hundred troopers as an advance party. Captain Mitchell followed with three hundred more. The storm virtually blinded the men and horses. Troopers fell asleep in their saddles, horses following each other automatically. Local Rebels had dropped large trees in the road to delay their passage. When Dahlgren ordered a halt to confer with Mitchell, he was not behind them. Scouts sent out could not find the three hundred men. Dahlgren, his forces split and out of touch, in enemy territory, in a storm, in the dark, with local bushwhackers all around, was in deep trouble.

By 8:00 a.m., Dahlgren's smaller force reached the high-running Pamunkey River and made their way across. By 2:00 p.m. he had struck another river, the Mattaponi, and had gotten half his force across when a local home guard saw them and fired upon them. Young Dahlgren sat his horse amid the whizzing bullets and directed his rear guard, fighting a delaying action until the rest of his men had gotten across the river. He crossed last.

Although they were moving closer to their objective of Fort Monroe, or possibly finding Kilpatrick, they were going deeper into enemy territory. And the locals knew they were there.

Part of a regular Confederate Army unit and their commander were in the area. Lt. James Pollard and some of his 9th Virginia Cavalry were supplemented with local home guards: farmers, preachers, schoolteachers, even a thirteen-year-old student, who would later be the cause of one of the biggest scandals of the war. The CSA regulars accompanied by their local contingent of home guardsmen rode hard and got ahead of Dahlgren's now-diminished column of seventy men.

Dahlgren's troopers' ammunition was almost gone; some were wounded; all were hungry and tired beyond endurance. Still, they rode on through the darkness onto a road constricted on each side by fences.

There was a sound. The column stopped. Dahlgren and a few others rode to the front of the men.

"Who are you?" one shouted. There was no answer from the darkness.

Dahlgren ordered, "Surrender, or we will shoot you."

From the side of the road, not fifteen feet away, a volley of musketry flashed and roared. Horses shied and panicked. Men and animals dropped into the muddy road. A Confederate prisoner had the presence of mind to tear down some of the fence, and the frightened, disorganized troopers poured through into a field.

In the now-quiet darkness, the schoolboy, William Littlepage, crept out to try to find a gold watch on one of the dead. He returned with a cigar case and a notebook, which he gave to his schoolteacher, Mr. Halbach. The teacher turned down the cigars, but kept the notebook and papers to read in the daylight. Littlepage then casually mentioned that the dead man from which he'd taken the notebook had a wooden leg. A Rebel who had just been a prisoner of the Yankees told them they had better get rid of the notebook and papers, because they had just killed Colonel Dahlgren, and would hang if the papers were found on them. Halbach still wanted to know what was in them, so he kept them until dawn.

In the daylight, what he read shocked him, so he passed the papers on to his superior, who showed them to Pollard. From there they went all the way up the chain of command to Confederate president Jefferson Davis.

What was in the papers that made them so incendiary? Keep in mind that nineteenth-century warfare had rules, although the American Civil War, with its outright war on civilians for no other reason than that they resided in the South, would go a long way toward changing those rules. One of the rules stated that kidnapping an enemy political leader was legal; killing an enemy political leader was beyond the pale.

The papers Dahlgren carried on the raid were written on official stationery, with "Headquarters Third Division, Cavalry Corps" printed at the top. Included was an address to the men of his command, signed "U. Dahlgren, Col. Comd." The address was pretty standard in that it outlined the goals of the mission, including releasing the prisoners from Belle Isle. But one of the goals had not been discussed with the planners of the raid—or at least, had not been recorded as having been discussed: "exhorting the released prisoners to destroy & burn the hateful City & do not allow the Rebel Leader Davis and his traitorous crew to escape."

It got worse. On another sheet with the same heading, in the same handwriting, were the words, "& once in the City it must be destroyed & Jeff. Davis and Cabinet killed." As well, in Dahlgren's notebook was found a draft of the address to the troops, and the directive, "Jeff Davis and Cabinet must be killed on the spot."

Around noon on March 4, Pollard arrived in Richmond with the papers and Dahlgren's wooden leg, perhaps as proof of their authenticity. He presented them to Robert E. Lee's nephew, cavalry commander Maj. Gen. Fitzhugh Lee. Lee took them to President Davis, who seemed to laugh off the threat in the papers. Others in his government did not find them amusing in the least.

To many, political assassination of an enemy's president broke all rules of civilized warfare. These papers were proof that the United States now intended to wage unrestricted war. They could only imagine the fate of their capital had Dahlgren succeeded: burned, looted, its women raped by depraved, released Yankee prisoners of war, their legally elected officials murdered in the halls of their capitol. The reporters were called in and the papers were released to show what sort of savage, uncivilized enemy the Southerners were now facing. The papers were even sent to London. The scandal went international.

While the contretemps grew, Kilpatrick, never wanting publicity to go to waste, wrote in his report that he was now determined to "visit the neighborhood" where Dahlgren had been killed, and exact revenge. Led by Gen. Isaac Wistar, 2,700 infantry and 1,100 cavalry arrived to burn King and Queen Court House, the village nearest the ambush site. Wistar ordered Kilpatrick back to Fort Monroe as worthless. Kilpatrick still claimed credit, saying the people of King and Queen Court House had been well punished by his cavalry.

On March 30, the papers were sent under a flag of truce to the Union Army commanders: Was Dahlgren acting under the orders of his government? Meade ordered Kilpatrick to investigate.

So, the fox investigated the chicken coop, and, lo and behold, declared that he had seen the address and endorsed it as "approved" in red ink, although at that time it had contained none of the inflammatory remarks. He claimed that this part of it was false—that the papers had been tampered with after he had "approved" them, thus starting the rumor that went on to feed the Northern newspapers, and dropping all the blame on the brave, youthful, and now-dead Dahlgren.

Meade, because of Kilpatrick's reputation, and the "collateral evidence" which he possessed, did not believe Kilpatrick's story. Others did not either, and also referred to "Kill-Cavalry's" tarnished reputation and conversations with Dahlgren by an officer who had survived the raid. It seemed like everyone in the army involved with the misbegotten raid wanted the subject dropped.

Not so the admiral. John Dahlgren, grief-stricken at the loss of his son, was moved to rage by the innuendo, even announcing his belief that the last name in the signature had been misspelled as "Dalhgren," something his son obviously would not do. This was debunked by later writers pointing out that the admiral had seen a lithograph copy of the address from Europe, one which showed a "bleed-through" of ink from the back of the paper, making the signature look misspelled. Twentieth-century historians also pointed out that the lithographer had retouched the signature.

Historians have since argued whether the papers were a complete forgery—belied by the chain of evidence, and the lack of time between Dahlgren's death and the time they were printed in Richmond's papers. Not to mention the long list of prominent people (as well as average individuals) who would have had to lie about their authenticity, then keep it a secret the rest of their lives, including a schoolboy who was just looking to snag himself a fancy watch.

Some Confederates broadened the effects of the papers found on Dahlgren. If the Yankee government was willing to assassinate the Confederate president and all the heads of a legitimate government, surely they had turned to a new type of warfare: "barbarous and inhuman," as Robert E. Lee called it. Some historians have postulated that the Confederate Secret Service felt it gave them carte blanche to put forth their plot to kidnap Lincoln. Some have linked John Wilkes Booth to the Confederate Secret Service through money exchanged. At the last minute, after Appomattox, Booth, apparently on his own, changed his plan from kidnapping to killing the president.

So how far up into the Federal government did the plot to decapitate the Confederate government go? Some historians discount the proposal that Dahlgren hatched the assassination plot himself. Too young, too low in rank, and, probably more importantly, from a military family, he knew how vital it was to get permission from one's "higher-ups." Kilpatrick? Historians who have studied his personality and career say that, after the "Buckland Races," and the personal loss of his family, thinking of higher aspirations (perhaps even running for president someday), he felt he needed something huge upon which to hang his hat. Having just gotten Lincoln's go-ahead for his plan (minus the assassination part), he then went to Secretary of War Stanton on February 12, 1864. Did the plan change then?

Stanton's hatred for Davis and the Confederacy is legendary. Add to that the fact that, after the war, when the Dahlgren papers lay in the captured Confederate archives, Stanton specifically requested to see them. From that day on, the originals vanished. Up in the smoke of Stanton's chimney, some speculate.

Finally, Meade, after the Kilpatrick/Dahlgren fiasco and its aftermath, rid himself and the Army of the Potomac of Kilpatrick, sending him to William T. Sherman's command farther south. Even Sherman knew about Kilpatrick's reputation. When warned about him before his march to the sea, he admitted, "I know that Kilpatrick is a hell of a damned fool, but I want just that sort of a man to command my cavalry on this expedition."

While with Sherman, Kilpatrick managed to nearly be captured in his underwear while with a prostitute. Later, he got his laundress pregnant. In South Carolina, the story goes that he held a ball for the local ladies. As they danced, he had his men set fire to all their homes. He got caught in his drawers again by raiding Confederates, this time in Columbia, and with a different woman.

Then there was "Charley," a woman who wore an army uniform and accompanied Kilpatrick to his bed, in spite of the pregnant laundress.

Judson Kilpatrick, the "hell of a damned fool," was lucky not to have been drummed out of the service. He seemed to survive because he was just what the army needed at just the right time, although for hundreds of young men who served under his command, including Elon J. Farnsworth and Ulric Dahlgren, his presence in the Union Army was most certainly a curse.

22

WILMER MCLEAN: FOLLOWED BY A CURSE

Wilmer McLean had done well in his life. By age forty-six, he had partnered with another man and established a successful retail-wholesale grocery business. He had married well, to a wealthy widow who had a large house on a beautiful plantation, with a slow, meandering stream nearby, called Bull Run. Fourteen slaves helped to run the farm. But by July of 1861, McLean could tell that something was about to change.

For a while now, troops from the newly formed Confederate Army had been encamping around his fields and the junction of the Orange and Alexandria and Manassas Gap Railroads. Since the fall of Fort Sumter in South Carolina in April, and the separation of the two sections of the country, some 21,000 Southern troops had marched on the junction. Another 11,000 were mustered in the Shenandoah Valley, awaiting orders.

All of these troops within about thirty miles of Washington made President Abraham Lincoln nervous. As well, the railroad junction at Manassas would provide a supply link to a Federal army on any offensive thrust on Richmond, the capital of the Confederacy.

Lincoln ordered Federal general Irvin McDowell to take the 35,000 troops from Washington and march on the Confederates at Manassas, to drive them from the area before they could be reinforced. He also gave orders to other Union forces to keep the

Confederates in the Shenandoah Valley under Gen. Joseph E. Johnston from joining those at Manassas.

Although he was doing a good business supplying the Confederate Army with sugar, McLean, a former officer in the Virginia militia, could read the movements of the two armies. He was not happy about the buildup around his "Yorkshire Plantation," so evacuated his wife and five children from the area, which turned out to be a good thing. But only temporarily.

By mid-July, the Union Army was on the march to Manassas, and the Confederate "Hero of Fort Sumter," Gen. P. G. T. Beauregard, had established his headquarters in the McLean house at Yorkshire Plantation. On July 18, a Union artillery shell burst in the fireplace of the kitchen of McLean's house—a lucky shot, no doubt—and spoiled the Confederate commander's meal. On July 21, the Union Army attacked the Confederates in what was to become the first major battle of the American Civil War.

Both sides were convinced they would be victorious. McDowell had created a battle plan that involved feints and flank marches to take advantage of his numerical superiority. Had he been commanding an army of veterans instead of fresh recruits, he may have been successful in making the complicated maneuvers required. As it turned out, the Confederates in the Valley had given the slip to the Union troops that were supposed to watch them, boarding trains and arriving at Manassas junction far faster than they would have marching. Their arrival and reinforcement of their fellow Confederates was the first time in history the railroads were used to deliver troops to a battlefield.

As well, even this early in the war, Confederates had a spy network set up in Washington, so Beauregard had been informed of his enemy's movements. Not that it mattered. Even he must have been surprised at how long it took the Union Army to march the thirty-odd miles from the capital to the battlefield of Manassas. New recruits took advantage of halts along the way to fill canteens, breaking ranks to pick blackberries. By the time they got to within five miles of the

Confederates, they had halted again, out of rations, to wait for more food to arrive.

Meanwhile, McDowell's plans had to be changed; Confederate positions at the proposed site of his initial attack convinced him it was too strong, and so he switched to concentrating on the other flank. It took two days to scout and have the battle plan redrawn.

A stone bridge across Bull Run was where the Federals began their feint around dawn. It was a fine demonstration against the troops of Col. Nathan G. Evans, but curiously, they never pressed their advantage. Soon Evans got a message via flag semaphore from signal officer E. P. Alexander: "Look to your left. You are turned." It confirmed Evans's suspicions that this initial attack was meant to distract him from the Federals' real intentions. He left a token force to oppose the Yankees at the bridge and marched to the real point of attack, at Matthews Hill.

Though he was outnumbered two to one, Evans delayed the Federal attack for two hours. One of the commanders of the Federal attack would, within the next two years, have his name both associated with victory in the North and used as a curse in the South, especially Georgia: William Tecumseh Sherman. Even after being reinforced, the Confederates were forced to withdraw up the slope of Henry Hill, named for the elderly woman whose house occupied it. Unlike Wilmer McLean, bedridden octogenarian Judith Henry refused to leave her home. A stray shell burst within it and killed her.

As the Confederates withdrew grudgingly, one of their commanders, Gen. Bernard Bee, saw the troops, commanded by a Virginia Military Institute professor, formed in line behind his retreating soldiers. "There stands Jackson like a stone wall. Rally behind the Virginians!" Historians quibble about whether he was cursing Thomas J. Jackson for not advancing to his aid, or admiring how well he kept his men cool under fire. Bee was killed shortly after his observation, so no one could ask him what he meant. What he did do, however, was give to the annals of military history a nom de guerre for the ages. From now on, the dowdy professor would be known as "Stonewall" Jackson, and his unit, "The Stonewall Brigade."

After a noontime lull in the fighting, McDowell would attack the Confederates again on Henry Hill, with little success, after which he would order a withdrawal back across Bull Run.

The Union troops had so far accounted for themselves admirably. In spite of being "short-timers"—near the end of their ninety-day enlistment—they had stood the fire of enemy infantry small arms and artillery and maneuvered on a confusing, smoke-filled battlefield, watching their comrades wounded and killed within arm's reach. But as they began their retreat, fate seemed to conspire against them.

Orderly at first, the withdrawal rapidly grew catastrophic. First there were the civilians and congressmen who had come out from Washington with their wine and picnic lunches to observe their soldiers' victory over the miscreant Rebels. As the Federal troops began streaming back toward them, they realized something was wrong; they began to leave their picnics, clogging the road back to the capital. Then there was the bottleneck at the Cub Run Bridge, exacerbated by a Confederate shell overturning a wagon in the middle of it. As Union troops waited to cross, a horrid rumor began making its way down the frozen column: The Confederates had unleashed one of their most diabolical weapons. Their fearsome "Black Horse Cavalry" was pounding down the road behind them, shooting, sabering, and riding down every Federal soldier in sight. With all these factors in play, the once-systematic retreat became a rout.

A few Union units maintained their composure, enough to discourage the Confederates, exhausted and disorganized in their own right, from a full pursuit to the gates of Washington.

Casualties, at least for that early in the war, appalled the nation: Confederates lost 1,750; the Union suffered 2,950 killed, wounded, and missing. As was soon to be seen, it was only the beginning.

In the meantime, Wilmer McLean was proved to have made the right choice in moving his family out of Yorkshire Plantation. Leaving his family, he returned to find that his barn had been commandeered by the surgeons and was now a hospital, with the wounded from both Union and Confederate sides scattered about the floor. He was probably glad he had not exposed his wife and children to the unspeakable horrors occurring in that structure.

He stayed, however, and worked as a Confederate quartermaster–appropriate for a professional grocery supplier–through February 1862. Come springtime, he reunited with his family.

But as if the war had some sort of personal grudge against Wilmer McLean, fighting came once again to the Manassas area of Virginia, a little more than a year later.

Shortly after the Battle of Bull Run (called the Battle of Manassas by the Confederates), Lincoln called on Gen. George B. McClellan to lead the Federal Army of the Potomac. In the spring of 1862, after much drilling and reorganization, his army was driven from the gates of Richmond and back down the Virginia Peninsula by Gen. Robert E. Lee, who had taken over the Confederate Army when Joseph E. Johnston was wounded. Gen. John Pope was appointed commander of the Federal Army of Virginia, and threatened the vital rail junction at Gordonsville, Virginia, to the northwest of Richmond.

The summer of 1862 saw a series of bold maneuvers from both armies. Northern leaders tried to unite McClellan's army from the Peninsula with Pope's army. Lee took the inside track. Calculating how long it would take for McClellan's Army of the Potomac to travel by boat down the James, through the Chesapeake Bay and along the Potomac, then march overland to get to Pope, Lee knew he could attack Pope before he could be reinforced.

Lee sent Jackson–now commanding a corps in Lee's army–with his 24,000 men marching on a loop to cover over fifty miles in just two days. They reached Manassas and found Federal supplies stockpiled at the junction. First, the always-hungry Confederate soldiers ate all they could; then they packed up all they could possibly carry; then they burned anything that could be used by the Federals.

As if cursed to be a killing ground, the land around Manassas junction and Wilmer McLean's home was to be soaked with human blood a second time. On the evening of August 28, knowing that James Longstreet's Corps was within a few hours' march, and that the setting sun would end hostilities before he could get into too much trouble, Stonewall Jackson picked a fight with one of the toughest units in the Union Army.

Near the Brawner Farm, a mile or so from the 1861 battlefield of Manassas, Jackson's men and units from the American Midwest—who would soon earn the title "The Iron Brigade"—started what could be called an old-fashioned, stand-up fight. While the rifle-musket commonly used by both armies is sometimes thought of today as primitive, though it took longer to load, it was every bit as deadly as modern weaponry. Tactical range was about three hundred yards, although the bullet fired from the Springfield or Enfield shoulder arms could kill at double that distance. The majority of the fighting at the Brawner Farm that sultry August evening took place between 80 and 150 yards. As the sun crawled to the horizon, more units entered the fight and fired at virtually point-blank range. Each side took tremendous casualties as they approached each other, sometimes as close as fifty yards, pouring volley after volley into packed ranks. The right flank of the Union line was fired upon from thirty yards away. Darkness finally forced an end to one of the fiercest and most intense battles of the war to date. Yet it was only prologue to what was to come.

Jackson retreated to an abandoned railroad bed and ensconced his remaining twenty thousand men there. At 5:30 a.m. on August 29, the main Federal assaults began. Jackson's job was to hold off twice as many Federals as he had Confederates until Longstreet arrived. Even after Longstreet connected with Jackson's line, Stonewall bore the brunt of the Union assaults. Fortunately for the Confederates, afternoon attacks were poorly coordinated. One whole Union Corps didn't even get into the fight. Nightfall ended the fighting that day.

Pope began to believe from erroneous reports that Jackson was beginning a retreat. Thinking all that was ahead of him was a mop-up and pursuit of defeated Confederates, he launched an attack on the afternoon of August 30. Advancing to the railroad bed, all thoughts of an easy day ahead were demolished by volleys from Jackson's men, determined to hold their position. Fighting was particularly savage at a section of the railroad embankment called "Deep Cut." Federals nearly broke through the Rebel lines at a place called "The Dump," when the Confederates ran out of ammunition. Still as fiercely determined to hold their positions as always, the Rebels pitched rocks at the advancing Union troops and drove them back as would have their ancestor warriors thousands of years before.

A hasty, mistaken withdrawal left a gap in the Union lines, leaving Lt. Charles Hazlett's battery of artillery the lone defenders of that area. Hazlett, realizing his predicament, sent an aide to find some infantry support. The aide brought back two Zouave regiments, the 10th and 5th New York, dressed in their garish red pantaloons, white gaiters, and tasseled fezzes, a throwback to the early days of the war when some units dressed in the style of the French army in Morocco. Hazlett's artillerists and the approximately 1,000 gaudy Zouave targets were attacked by Longstreet's 28,000 veteran soldiers. Needless to say, the slaughter was horrendous.

Longstreet's assault pushed all the way toward Henry Hill, and the Union troops withdrew before them after blunting Longstreet's attack. Sunset brought an end to the fighting.

Casualties for the 70,000 Union troops who fought totaled 14,450. From the Confederate's 55,000 engaged, lost as killed, wounded, and missing were 9,400.

As far as Wilmer Mclean was concerned, he'd had enough.

In the fall of 1863, he moved his family southwest 120 miles, out of the field of combat and away from the seat of war. He bought a beautiful house that was once a tavern along the Lynchburg-Richmond Stage Road. The Southside Railroad which ran to Petersburg was nearby, and he employed it in his grocery business, still supplying the Confederate Army with sugar.

But McLean, like most Southerners in 1864, must have realized that the war was going badly for the Confederates. After fighting through the Wilderness west of Fredericksburg, the Confederate Army of Northern Virginia under Robert E. Lee found itself with its back to the capital, Richmond. The summer of 1864 saw the Southern army engaged in siege warfare as its lines were increasingly stretched thinner and thinner, trying to protect both Richmond and Petersburg, thirty miles to the south. Slowly over the winter, the Federals extended their lines around Petersburg, and in the early spring began a campaign to the west, stretching the Confederate line to its breaking point.

But up until this time, the Southside Railroad ran into Petersburg and Wilmer McLean, after having had battles literally in his backyard, must have thought his personal curse of the Civil War had worn off. But fate wasn't done with him yet.

On April 1, 1865, combined Federal infantry and cavalry attacks on a strategic road intersection called Five Forks to the southwest of Petersburg changed everything.

Five Forks, as the name implies, was the intersection of five significant roads vital on the supply route to the rear of the Confederate Army, ensconced at Petersburg. Not only did the roads lead to the Confederate lines, but they also allowed the Confederates to block the way to one of the main supply lines to Petersburg, the Southside Railroad just a few miles to the north.

Maj. Gen. Philip Sheridan, the feisty commander of Union commanding general Ulysses S. Grant's cavalry, was in a seriously foul mood prior to the battle. He had been given overall command of the operation by Grant and wanted to get things moving quickly, cavalry-style, but felt he was being held up by the slogging infantry. In particular, he kept in the back of his mind Maj. Gen. Gouverneur K. Warren.

Warren had a reputation as "The Savior of Little Round Top" at Gettysburg, after having discovered its vulnerability and ordered Union troops to it just moments before Confederates attacked. Since then, he had been given the command of the Fifth Corps, and had fought well in the battles since, while still maintaining a reputation as a very cautious general. To Sheridan, as he stood surrounded by officers of the Fifth Corps, who would soon carry out his aggressive orders to assault the entrenched Confederates at Five Forks, that was ancient history. *Now* was all that mattered to Sheridan, and the sun seemed to him to race across the sky toward the west. In the middle of a dirt road in front of a tiny rural church, called Gravelly Run Episcopal Church, he drew his sword and carved his battle plan into the very soil of the enemy.

At 4:15 p.m., the 12,000 men of the Fifth Corps began their assault upon Five Forks. The charge was impulsive confusion, but did the job and broke the Confederate lines in classic nineteenth-century military fashion: flags waving and horses leaping the earthworks. Sheridan, however, wondered where Warren was.

He hadn't forgotten Warren's criticizing his "damned cavalry" for clogging his route and getting in his way as he tried to march during the fighting in the Wilderness. Recently, Sheridan had found him sleeping in his tent in the middle of the afternoon, depressed about the high casualty rates, among other things. When he hadn't shown up with his corps on time (according to Sheridan's timetable) just a few days before, Sheridan had blamed Warren, and not the difficulty of a nighttime march, high streams, muddy roads, and delayed marching orders from Grant. Even after Sheridan had issued his orders for the attack on Five Forks, Warren, ever the engineer, sat down under a tree to sketch the terrain. Sheridan fumed.

Even after the victory was won at Five Forks and his men had rounded up some five thousand prisoners, he was still mad at Warren. Asking where he was and told he was in the Confederate rear, Sheridan concluded he was "not at the front," where officers should be, and relieved him of command. Warren in a pitiful gesture finally approached Sheridan and asked him to reconsider. "Reconsider, hell! I don't reconsider my decisions," Sheridan said in typical Sheridan fashion. "Obey the order."

Warren would waste much of the rest of his life attempting to restore his good reputation, cursed—literally—by the impulsive Sheridan.

When Grant received word of Sheridan's success, he ordered a general assault of four Union corps all along the Petersburg front.

The next afternoon, April 2, the Confederates fought a losing battle about three miles to the north, to keep the Southside Railroad open. As they attempted to repulse the main Union assaults along their Petersburg lines, Lee sent a message to Confederate president Jefferson Davis, recommending the evacuation of Richmond. It was now just a matter of time for the Confederacy.

Lee led his army westward in an attempt to escape Grant's fast-moving cavalry and infantry, and to connect with Joseph Johnston's Confederate army in North Carolina. Historians have called it "the week of running fights." Brig. Gen. Joshua L. Chamberlain, who marched with the Fifth Corps on the last campaign, wrote, "There was blood at every bridge and ford." Lee's first priority was to feed his half-starved army. The Federals would try to make that impossible.

Nearly everywhere Lee thought he might get rations, Sheridan's cavalry beat him there. Marching parallel to Lee, they struck when they could, rounding up weak, straggling prisoners, and burning wagons when the opportunities presented themselves. George Armstrong Custer was with Sheridan's cavalry and broke the Confederate column, burning several hundred wagons. At Sayler's Creek in a battle there, as he watched thousands of his soldiers surrendering, Lee thought his army had been dissolved.

Finally Lee headed to where he had ordered boxcars full of rations: Appomattox Station.

Custer got there first, on April 8. He overran the Confederate force and captured the trains, sending them away down the tracks. Preliminary correspondence had begun between Lee and Grant, expressing the desire to end additional "effusion of blood."

More troops arrived at the small village, and armies once again found Wilmer McLean, who must have wondered just what he had done wrong to deserve having a war follow him through Virginia. By April 9, 1865, after a futile dawn attack to attempt to break out, Lee realized he was all but surrounded. There was only one thing left for him to do. As the always combative Lee stated, "I would rather die a thousand deaths."

Remarkably, Grant allowed Lee to choose the place of surrender. Lee's trusted aide Charles Marshall found a large building among the twenty or so in the village of Appomattox Court House. Marshall rejected a run-down structure and picked a larger, brick building with a roomy parlor that seemed suitable for the austere ceremony that was to take place: the surrender of the famed Army of Northern Virginia.

The house belonged to none other than Wilmer McLean, formerly of Manassas, Virginia. The war had seemingly stalked him, beginning in his backyard and virtually ending in his parlor.

Though the war did not end with Lee's surrender—as there were other Confederate armies in existence in the South and across the Mississippi—the surrender at Appomattox signaled that the South could no longer sustain itself against the onslaught of Federal forces. Joseph E. Johnston surrendered his Army of Tennessee in North Carolina on April 26, 1865; the last land battle took place in Texas, near Brownsville, at Palmetto Ranch, on May 12 and 13, 1865; and the Rebel raider CSS *Shenandoah*, isolated on the high seas, finally surrendered in November, 1865, in Liverpool, England.

After Lee and Grant left McLean's parlor, Union officers and enlisted men practically looted the house of anything remotely connected to the surrender: Tables, chairs, knickknacks, candlesticks, even a stuffed doll belonging to Lula, McLean's young daughter, left in the parlor as a "silent witness," all began to vanish from McLean's house, some paid for, some not. Wilmer McLean, according to one eyewitness, was already in a high state of excitement, "shaking his system to its nervous center," and it certainly didn't help his agitation when he saw his furnishings disappearing.

After the war and the drying up of his grocery supply business to the Confederate army (and perhaps the nonpayment of the bill from the now-defunct Confederacy, or their payment in now-worthless Confederate scrip), the McLeans left Appomattox and returned to what was left of Yorkshire, near Manassas, in 1867. McLean defaulted on loans, and the banks in Richmond foreclosed on him. His house at Appomattox, where one of the more-important moments in American history occurred, was sold at public auction on November 29, 1869. McLean ended up moving to Alexandria and working for the Internal Revenue Service, perhaps becoming a curse himself on his taxpaying contemporaries.

23

ROBERT E. LEE: CURSED VIRGINIAN?

Robert E. Lee's name resides imperishably in the pantheon of notable, famous, respected Virginians of the past. Before he was even born his family was known simply as "The Lees of Virginia," and boasted connections with the earliest, wealthiest aristocracy of the state. His mother was Ann Hill Carter, great-granddaughter of the renowned Robert "King" Carter, once the largest landowner in Virginia, and a rich tobacco baron. Lee's father, "Light Horse" Harry Lee, was a Revolutionary War hero and personal friend of George Washington.

As a general, Robert E. Lee is remembered as the battlefield leader of the noble "Lost Cause," whose reputation, even though he failed to win his country's independence, remains stainless. He is the one man whose name adorns the high school diplomas of millions all across the South.

Why, then, would he be included in a book about Virginia's cursed?

Consider it a tribute to his character. Many historians believe there is a reason why he has been so admired since the end of the Civil War. It's called "good PR."

Not that, in most cases, he doesn't deserve a stellar reputation. But the faction writing about him after his death had a tendency to overstate some of his qualities, in some cases giving him nearly supernatural powers of prescience. Of course, this embellishment of his character after his death is not Lee's doing. Making Lee seem godlike suited the postwar Confederates' purposes of self-defense, but also, in a backhanded way, took away from the real Lee, and the personal challenges he had to overcome in order to achieve the status he eventually gained.

He was born into one of America's most prominent families, descended from Richard Lee I, called "The Emigrant," who settled in the Northern Neck of Virginia (between the Potomac and Rappahannock Rivers) and, in 1641, began to build an empire based upon land ownership. He was a planter and merchant, and owned his own fleet of ships with which to trade well outside of Virginia. He also served in the General Assembly.

Robert E. Lee's father, born in 1756, became a high-ranking soldier in Washington's Continental Army, as well as a good friend of the first president, in spite of the fact that his mother, apparently a beauty even at the age of fifteen, turned down George Washington's proposal of marriage. In the Revolution Harry Lee soon won the nom de guerre of "Light Horse" Harry, for his exploits with light cavalry. Harry was well-educated, entering Princeton at fifteen. Sensing the growing uneasiness between Britain and her colonies in America, instead of studying law in London he stayed home and engaged with youthful exuberance in the party scene at the nearby plantations.

When war with Britain broke out, Harry joined the Virginia Light Dragoons, cavalry armed only with horse pistols and short swords, used for quick dashes at the enemy to gather information and harass. Later, after the army-wide torture of Valley Forge, he was transferred south to fight with Nathanael Greene. There he commanded "Lee's Legion."

Like many young men who find great success in military affairs, when the war ended, Light Horse Harry, at age twenty-five, was lost. Returning to the Northern Neck, he courted and married a nineteen-year-old second cousin named Matilda Ludwell Lee, whom he had known all her life. They settled in her family's extraordinary plantation mansion, Stratford Hall. But after the life of a cavalier, he found running a plantation boring.

Light Horse Harry began to speculate in land, eventually pouring much of his wife's fortune into land over which a great canal would be built along the Potomac. Unfortunately for Lee, the canal wouldn't be built until twenty-three years after his death. Sadly, while his speculating was going on and his selling off of her land continued, Matilda died after placing Stratford and other lands in a trust for her children. Harry's reputation as being terrible with money became universal in a society that valued land husbandry above all else.

While his reputation with money was shot, with his ebullient personality he was still well-liked. Even though his financial situation was pitiful, his social standing still rose, especially with his colleagues in the General Assembly, who elected and then reelected him to three one-year terms as governor of Virginia. After Matilda's death, he escaped from what he considered the boredom of being governor in Richmond to the plantations along the James River, and the social life they offered.

Harry was thirty-seven and courting her cousin when twenty-year-old Ann Hill Carter grew infatuated with the dashing, personable Revolutionary War hero and governor of Virginia. When her cousin turned down his proposal, Ann made her feelings known, so Harry proposed to her.

Once married, they resided at Stratford Hall. It was there that they lost their first child at fifteen months of age. By the time Ann was thirty, she had borne three children, Charles Carter, Sydney Smith, and Ann. She wrote to her sister-in-law that she wanted no more children. Light Horse Harry was often gone from her side on political and military duties, and she frequently spent time away from Stratford Hall at the Tidewater plantations of her youth.

Meanwhile, Harry was up to his old tricks, selling off their land, speculating, and even paying off a debt to his old friend and mentor, George Washington, with devalued bank shares. Creditors came knocking on the massive, magnificent doors of Stratford Hall, demanding payment for Lee's debts. Perhaps it was the stress of having to send them away, but Ann soon began to suffer from debilitating illnesses doctors could not put their fingers on.

In 1806 she discovered she was pregnant again. She took their rickety old carriage (the only transportation Light Horse Harry could afford) to her childhood plantation home of Shirley, arriving in time to learn of the death of her father. She was brokenhearted; her husband was on the run from creditors and, according to some historians, she was about to have a child she did not want.

She returned to a bleak, wintry Stratford Hall and an ill husband. Here she was: in mourning, physically ill, anxious about her husband's debts and his health, and him about to go on the run again from the debtors. This was her psychological makeup when, on January 19, 1807, she gave birth to another son, whom she named after her brothers, Robert Edward Lee.

Though Stratford Hall was in slow, quiet decay, Robert still enjoyed a happy childhood with his siblings. Periodically Henry, his older stepbrother from his father's first marriage, would visit from his college, William and Mary in Williamsburg.

Robert would see another younger sister, Mildred, born. Although he inherited some of his father's traits (in particular, his utter oblivion to danger), his mother would be his guiding influence since, when Robert was merely two, his father was thrown into debtors' prison for a year. During his incarceration, he was moved from the Westmoreland County jail to the Spotsylvania County jail—a place name that would one day figure largely in his son Robert's military career.

While Robert may not have been wanted, he soon became arguably his mother's favorite child, filling the void left by the death, in a short period of time, of her father, brother, and closest sister.

Robert was four years old when the family moved, due to the difficulties of running such a large mansion, from the great and spacious Stratford Hall to a small, two-story house in Alexandria, Virginia. Even though their location had changed, visitors and neighbors reminded Robert of his lineage. Living in Alexandria was a constant reminder of his boyhood hero, George Washington, whose descendants called the town on the Potomac home, and into whose family Lee would eventually marry.

The War of 1812 brought Light Horse Harry a commission in the army, but happenstance leapt in the way of rejuvenating his career in the military. While visiting a publisher friend in Baltimore, Lee got involved in a brawl over something his friend had published. He was beaten so badly by the mob that he was left for dead. Slowly recovering in Alexandria, in 1813, with the financial help of well-placed friends, he boarded a ship for Barbados in order to fully recover his health. Robert would never see his father again. The Revolutionary War hero would die in 1818, on his journey home, and be buried on Cumberland Island off the coast of Georgia.

With his chronically ill mother left as the sole manager of the household, Robert took over some of the duties. His bond with his mother was always strong, and historians have credited her with aligning his virtues: duty, responsibility, appreciation of family and heritage, love of nature and animals, self-control, and self-denial.

While he was growing up in Alexandria, his half-brother Harry, now the owner of Stratford Hall, returned and began to restore the plantation after marrying his wealthy neighbor Anne McCarty. Along with Anne came her teenage, orphaned sister, Elizabeth, to become Harry's ward. So Robert had opportunities to visit both Stratford Hall and Shirley Plantations as he grew into his teenage years, reminding him once again of the Lee heritage. One sordid event would occur, however, to curse the Lee family's reputation and follow Robert through much of his life.

In 1820, Henry and Anne's two-year-old daughter, while at play, fell down the massive stone steps of Stratford Hall and was killed. Anne, inconsolable, was given morphine to ease her emotional distress. Before long she was addicted. Thirty-three-year-old Harry, turned out from his wife's bedroom by her debilitating addiction, did the unthinkable in Virginia society: He allegedly seduced his nineteen-year-old sister-in-law. Those accusations grew more solid with the rumors of the birth of a stillborn child to Elizabeth. Soon, when Elizabeth's original guardian sued to get her away from Stratford Hall, the legal action made the affair public knowledge. In shame Elizabeth cut off all her hair as a gesture of mourning. All over Virginia, the son of Light Horse Harry Lee got the name that went along with his reputation: "Black Horse" Harry Lee. In a moment of lucidity, Anne left him. He sold Stratford and moved to Tennessee.

Probably through his mother, Robert learned from this family scandal the value of self-control and self-denial, as well as the virtue of financial economy. As he got older, his duties toward her as caretaker grew. He was seen carrying her in his arms to their carriage for her daily rides. His religious inclinations seem to stem from her training too: He grew to know her unquestioning faith in God's will, even when things did not seem to turn out for the better.

He attended some nearby private schools, and the teachers there praised his diligence. Even though he was the son of a high-ranking army officer, there is no record of him showing or expressing the desire to be a professional soldier when he was young. Perhaps it was financial necessity that led him to apply to the United States Military Academy at West Point, New York. It seems his mother's teachings would serve him well there.

He excelled in virtually all fields of endeavor at the academy, no doubt from the lessons of self-discipline taught by his mother. After four years he stood second in his class and had earned no demerits the entire time. Shortly after graduation, with Robert by her bedside, her long illnesses, which, in their own way helped him learn how to handle adversity with grace, finally took their toll. She died on July 10, 1829.

Duty called. As an officer in the Corps of Engineers, he began to build fortifications at Cockspur Island near Savannah, Georgia. On furlough, he returned to Virginia and met Mary Anne Randolph Custis, who happened to live in the magnificent columned mansion on the hill in Arlington that overlooked the nation's capital. She also happened to be the daughter of George Washington Parke Custis, the adopted relation of George Washington. The next year he proposed to her, and would officially became related (by marriage) to his boyhood hero on the last day of June, 1831. In August they moved to his next assignment, in Fort Monroe, Virginia, again to work with the engineers. In 1832, their first child was born, a son whom they named George Washington Custis, and Lee began to enjoy family life, which, as his life grew more complicated, would become one of his few sources of pleasure.

Work with the other engineers was tedious. In 1834, he and Mary had an opportunity to return to Arlington with his assignment to Washington. Mary was pleased to be back in her old home. On July 12, 1835, a daughter, Mary Custis, was born. Lee was not at Arlington, however, when the baby arrived. He had been sent on a special assignment to survey and settle a boundary dispute between Ohio and the Michigan Territory. Soon after giving birth, Mrs. Lee began suffering from various illnesses. When Lee returned, he must have been reminded of the invalid his mother had become, and no doubt wondered if it was happening all over again. A cousin of Lee's saw him and thought that he'd never seen a man so changed and saddened.

To add to his domestic problems, his career, in peacetime and in the engineers, was utterly stalled. In a letter to a friend he mentioned that he was looking for a good opportunity to resign from the army. Lee had been promoted to first lieutenant in 1836, but for being in the army seven years, it was not much of an advancement in rank, or pay.

By June, 1837, his wife's health had improved, and William Henry Fitzhugh was born to the Lees. They nicknamed him Rooney. Shortly after, Lee received orders, sending him to St. Louis to try to tame the meandering Mississippi, which was about to sink commercial enterprises in the river town. He was praised highly for his ingenious solutions to the problems presented by the mighty river, but personally missed his family. And he missed Virginia.

Ice on the river closed up shop for Lee's engineers, and he returned to his beloved state for the winter. In the spring he took Mary and the two boys back with him to St. Louis. In May of 1839, Mary was pregnant again, and Lee accompanied the family back to Arlington, but had to return immediately to his post in the West. In letters he expressed how much he missed his family. On June 15, 1839, Anne Carter Lee was born, with her father away in St. Louis.

When Lee was in St. Louis, he longed for his family to be with him, and also worried about their upbringing without their father present. Letters to his wife and his mother-in-law, with whom he had developed a close relationship, reveal his concerns about the children's lack of discipline and growing willfulness. However, circumstances prevented anything but winter visits to Arlington. The Mississippi project ended in the fall of 1840. On February 27, 1841, Eleanor Agnes Lee was born.

In 1841 Lee finally made captain and was sent to work on New York's harbor. His family went with him. Their quarters in Fort Hamilton were no Arlington, but they stayed there for five years, returning to Virginia for holidays and occasional duty in Washington, and, in 1843, to watch over the birth of another son, Robert E. Lee Jr.

Lee was affected in the extreme by childhood accidents to little Annie and Rooney. Annie had an accident to her eye that disfigured the young child. (Tellingly, historians have found no photographs of her.) Lee saw her grow more self-conscious about her appearance as she grew up and, in his will before going off to the Mexican War, he made special provisions for her. Rooney, playing with a straw-cutter in a moment of rebellion, permanently damaged two fingers. Lee sat up holding his son's hand for nights so it would heal while Rooney got some sleep. These accidents and the childish disobedience of his other children weighed heavily on him as they grew.

Like all men with a growing family, Lee was constantly worried about family finances. Always, in the back of his mind, loomed the fortunes squandered by his father and half-brother. His brother Carter often came up with investment opportunities for Robert, but was turned down. Robert worried about his older brother's poor financial decisions. Then, in the mid-1840s, an economic depression hit the country, and the army reduced officers' salaries, leaving Lee to believe he had never been poorer in his life.

Lee, approaching forty, with a large family and at the whim of the government as to where he would be living and working next, expressed in letters how old he was beginning to feel. In 1846, the United States declared war on Mexico, but for three months, Lee did not get the call, no doubt wondering if he would ever see action. Despite its dangers, combat was the only way to quick promotion.

Then in August, Lee got his orders to report for duty in Mexico. Oddly, for all the money worries Lee had expressed, the will he prepared before leaving for the war zone indicates that he had large investments in stocks and bonds. The annual income from these, he wrote his wife, should be enough to pay to educate the children.

At first he was assigned to engineering duties. Then, at the beginning of 1847, he was ordered to join Gen. Winfield Scott's staff, preparing for the campaign against Veracruz, considered by many to be the most formidable fort in this hemisphere. Lee helped to plan and participate in the first large-scale amphibious assault in American military history. Writing home about his action directing a battery of artillery firing into the town, however, he expressed concern about the women and children who could be hurt by the shelling.

Ordered on a reconnaissance mission, he went out alone—small, inconspicuous scouting parties would become his trademark in the future—nearly was captured, and had to spend all day hiding behind a log while Mexicans drank from a nearby spring, and even stepped over the log he was hiding behind. He later led an American division along the trail he had discovered, and turned the flank of the Mexican army, helping to win the victory at Cerro Gordo. For his actions he won high praise and a brevet promotion to major.

He had finally entered the crucible of combat as an officer, and had excelled. Not only that, but he learned from one of America's premier officers, General Scott. He returned to the United States to work in Washington, survey Florida, and work on Fort Carroll in the Patapsco River, defending the seaport of Baltimore. He entered one of the happiest periods of his life, spending evenings telling stories to his children and, of all things (remember, this is the great General Lee), having them tickle his feet.

In 1852 he was offered the superintendency of his alma mater, the US Military Academy at West Point. His son Custis was then a cadet at the Academy, eventually graduating first in his class of 1854. His nephew, Fitzhugh Lee, was also attending, along with a young cadet who eventually grew close to Lee's family, especially Mary Custis, a couple of years his junior. During the Civil War his name would eventually become engraved on the same granite of Confederate history as Lee's: J. E. B. ("Jeb") Stuart.

While at West Point, Lee's faithful correspondent, mentor, and mother-in-law, Mrs. Custis, died. Though his faith allowed him to concede that mourning her passage to a better world made no sense, he still missed her counsel.

As superintendent, he continually worried about the welfare of his cadets, even down to whether they were writing home to their parents often enough.

In the spring of 1855, after Congress created two new regiments of cavalry (lighter, more mobile versions of the old dragoon regiments), Lee was assigned to the 2nd Cavalry as a lieutenant colonel. Finally, a promotion. The drawback: The cavalry was stationed in Texas, where he would remain, with one exception, for the next five years. He felt, as he wrote his wife, that he was being punished for his sins.

While his daughters Annie and Agnes, much to their father's delight, experienced a commitment to religion, Rooney had failed to be admitted to West Point, and caused his father's concern over his lack of self-discipline. Soon he would leave Harvard to join the army and get married to Charlotte Wickham. Rooney's father found in her a new correspondent to take the place of his mother-in-law.

In October of 1857, Mary's father died, leaving Lee executor to his will. It was an extremely complicated affair which stretched Lee's leave-time from the army from two months to more than two years. George Washington Parke Custis's three plantations would go to Lee's sons; from their income, $10,000 would go to each of Lee's daughters. The problem was that the plantations were pretty run-down and needed much work in order to become profitable enough to do more than feed Lee's sons.

The other challenge for Lee was to pay the $10,000 in debts his father-in-law left. Most difficult was his order to emancipate his nearly two hundred slaves. All of the demands in the will were to be accomplished within five years of his death.

Lee's concern for his reputation was heightened by a series of letters to the *New York Tribune* in which Lee was depicted as personally whipping one of his inherited, runaway slaves. The letters went on to insinuate that G. W. P. Custis had fathered fifteen of his own slaves.

Sadly, the paper chose to print the letters, which were (perhaps tellingly) never signed.

In October of 1859, while still in Arlington, Lee was ordered to take a contingent of US Marines to Harpers Ferry to quell an intended slave insurrection led by abolitionist John Brown. Jeb Stuart, also on leave in Washington at the time, just happened to hear of Lee's assignment, and volunteered as an aide. Brown's efforts were ended, but his ensuing trial kept Lee from rejoining his unit in Texas until mid-February, 1860. At this point in his life, duty in Texas was not much better than the prospects at home.

Then, because of historic sectional difficulties between the Northern and Southern states, circumstances carried Robert E. Lee on an irresistible tide to his most memorable role.

Lee, of course, is remembered as the seemingly invincible general, never defeated on the battlefield, who had to yield only because he was overwhelmed by the vastly greater numbers and supplies of the enemy. A study of his military career, once the Civil War began, may tell a slightly different story.

First, he was not the dyed-in-the-wool Confederate some would like to see him as. Letters to his wife show that he feared dissolution of the Union, and blamed the coming war on "ambitious and selfish" politicians. In the early spring of 1861, he was recalled by the army to Washington. Upon returning to Arlington, he found his wife more debilitated than ever by her rheumatoid arthritis.

On April 18, 1861, Lee met his old Mexican War commander, Winfield Scott, who had been appointed general-in-chief of the army, and expressed the desire to have Lee as his second-in-command. Lee's next meeting was with Francis Blair, who spoke on behalf of the new president, Abraham Lincoln. The federal government was in the process of raising an army of 100,000 to enforce its laws upon the country, including the Southern states, which were in apparent rebellion against the government. They wanted Lee to command that army.

Lee replied that he was opposed to the secession of states from the Union, but turned down Blair's offer, citing that it would necessarily entail an invasion of the Southern states. The next day,

Virginia seceded from the Union, after originally voting against leaving the country. On April 20, he wrote his formal resignation from the United States Army, the career that had frustrated him for more than three decades. Considering he had turned down a promotion from regimental command to second-in-command of an entire army larger than was ever fielded in the history of the country, it was an incredible move.

In a letter to his sister Anne, who would remain loyal to the Union, he wrote that he was still devoted to the Union, still felt the duty of an American citizen, but he could not find it in his conscience to raise his hand "against my relatives, my children, my home."

He was now unemployed—but not for long. He was summoned to Richmond, the new capital of the newly formed Confederate States of America, where he accepted command of the state's troops. Considering his previously stalled career, the sudden offer by the US Army, his resignation, then the promotion to command Virginia's troops, his emotions must have been in turmoil. Add to this the fact that his home in Arlington, where his wife, daughters, and heirlooms of George Washington resided, was just across the Potomac from the Federal capital, and unprotected from invasion. He urged his wife to abandon the home. Mary and the Lee girls had to begin living with friends and relatives across Virginia until 1864, when they finally settled in Richmond.

Though he was given the command of Virginia troops, since they all had been mustered into the Confederate national army, Lee ended up at a desk job in Richmond. The fact that Jefferson Davis, president of the Confederacy, had graduated from West Point, was a Mexican War veteran, and had served as secretary of war under President Franklin Pierce, led him to meddle in military affairs much more than a nonmilitary-oriented politician.

In his role in Davis's administration, Lee missed out on the first major battle of the war, the Confederate victory at Manassas, Virginia. He wrote to his wife that he was "mortified" by his absence. When Confederate troops failed to follow up on their success, the public blamed Lee's strategy from Richmond, going so far as to claim it was affecting his marriage! To Mary, he called them "Vile slanderers."

In August, he finally got a field assignment: to control the Unionist-leaning western part of Virginia, which he did, until nearly winter. Between the Yankees and the population's sentiments, it was an impossible task. Eventually, western Virginia withdrew from the secession and was welcomed back into the Union as West Virginia. His next assignment was the coastal defenses of South Carolina. He must have thought his career had gone back in time thirty years. Finally, in the spring, he was recalled to Richmond. Though his duty there was to entail overall authority of military operations, Jeff Davis kept his hand in everything.

A new Northern commander, George B. McClellan, would change things. His grandiose plan was to land an invading Union army by ship at the Union-held tip of the Virginia Peninsula, march it past Jamestown, Williamsburg, through the swamps of the Chickahominy River, right up to Richmond, and capture the Confederate capital. As the Yankees moved up the Peninsula, Lee's wife Mary and daughters Annie and Mildred had to go on the run from Rooney's plantation, called "White House."

Opposing McClellan was Confederate general Joseph E. Johnston, who orchestrated a strategic retreat back toward Richmond. Lee offered his assistance to Johnston, but was told the only real assistance he could render was to find reinforcements. Things changed drastically, however, when on May 31, Johnston was wounded during the Battle of Seven Pines. Davis turned to his trusted aide Lee to take over. In addition to suddenly having to assume command of an army in mid-battle, he also learned that his wife and two daughters had been captured by the Federals.

By now, Richmonders were abandoning their capital; even Jefferson Davis's family had fled. On June 2, Lee was in the field when a carriage pulled up to his headquarters carrying his wife and two daughters who had, through the graciousness of the enemy commander, been allowed through the lines. It had been over a year since they had seen each other. The stress and worry had aged him as much as her arthritis had aged her. The meeting was brief, for Mary was heading for a safe house, and he had planning to do for his first battlefield command.

McClellan, by his nature, gave Lee plenty of time. He waited until June 25 to assault the Confederates at what would come to be called the Battle of Oak Grove. It was a tactical draw, but, as events would soon show, it signified the end of McClellan's advance toward Richmond, as well as Lee's emergence as the South's preeminent officer.

The next day Lee began his assaults that would convince McClellan to abandon his plans to take Richmond and withdraw back down the Peninsula. Though Stonewall Jackson was uncharacteristically late for the fight and Confederate general A. P. Hill attacked prematurely, the Battle of Mechanicsville was a strategic success for the Confederates, in that McClellan panicked and began what he euphemistically called his "change of base"—a retreat.

Several more battles were fought as McClellan withdrew. Called "The Seven Days' Battles," they demonstrated an interesting characteristic in Lee that few people had realized he possessed: audacity. Certainly his military career up until the point he took command of the Army of Northern Virginia had given him no chance to display his aggressiveness—building forts would give no opportunity for audacity—but now that he was in a command position, the trait would show through. And, according to several historians, like the main character in a Greek tragedy, it would turn out to be his hidden fatal flaw.

Churches, courthouses, and even private homes in and around Richmond filled to overflowing with wounded from the battles that saved the capital. Cemeteries did, too. The climax of the Seven Days' Battles was the Battle of Malvern Hill. The terrain leading to the Union position was open, swept by their field artillery, which was supported by the huge cannons on gunboats on the James River. Instead of utilizing roads which were out of sight and range of the big guns to flank the Federal position, Lee chose frontal assault. It confounded even his most loyal officers. Casualty figures back this up. Although the Seven Days' Battles is considered a victory for

Lee, his army suffered 21 percent casualties, as opposed to only 11 percent for McClellan. Sadly, those figures foretold a grim future for Lee's Army of Northern Virginia, and eventually, for the existence of the Confederacy.

Shortly after the Confederate catastrophe of Malvern Hill, another burial in Richmond struck Lee a heavy blow: His namesake grandson, Rooney's two-year-old son, Robert E. Lee, had died and was buried on July 5, 1862, in Shockoe Cemetery.

More personal tragedy stalked Lee while he shouldered the burden of army command that summer. In addition to losing his son, Rooney's "White House" was burned to the ground by Federal soldiers. Lee also learned that he had a new Union commander to face, one the normally reserved Lee called "a miscreant," John Pope. Pope was a bombastic braggart who threatened to execute any civilian caught aiding the Confederacy. Lee issued orders stating that Pope's officers, if captured, would be given the same treatment. That ended Pope's threat.

Again taking the offensive, Lee's army engaged Pope near the previously fought-over battlefield of Manassas. From the moment Jackson opened the battle at Groveton, at dusk on August 28, 1862, until evening halted Longstreet's final assault on August 30, Lee's army, though victorious, took 19 percent casualties to Pope's 13 percent. The lesson, according to historian Edward H. Bonekemper III, was obvious: Longstreet's three-hour attack cost Lee's army more men than Jackson's three days on the defense.

In addition, Lee had hurt his hands. His always active horse Traveller had spooked while Lee was dismounted. Trying to stop him, Lee tumbled down, catching himself on his hands but apparently spraining them and breaking some bones. It would limit his writing ability until the following spring, and probably affected his equestrian mobility for a while as well.

Although his army had suffered large losses in June and August of the summer of 1862, Lee was determined to launch an invasion of the Northern states. His stated objectives were to advance through Maryland, which he thought harbored Confederate sympathies, and move on into Pennsylvania, perhaps as far as the capital of Harrisburg.

The invasion did not go well. His men lacked proper provisions for an invasion; many were eating apples and raw corn; shoes were becoming scarce; desertions ran high; battle attrition had stripped his officer corps. He also divided his army with the enemy nearby. Then fate stepped in.

A Union soldier discovered three cigars wrapped in paper at a former Confederate campsite. The paper was a copy of Lee's orders for the invasion. Fortunately for Lee, the orders went immediately to McClellan, who now again opposed him. Any other commander would have used the information to destroy Lee's army piecemeal; McClellan dawdled with the intelligence.

The two armies squared off near Sharpsburg, Maryland, on September 17, 1862, with Lee's back to Antietam Creek. From dawn to dusk, the fighting resulted in the bloodiest single day in all of American history. As it developed, Lee missed having his army destroyed by the last-minute arrival of A. P. Hill's corps, in time to stop a massive Union assault. Though his army suffered incredibly high casualties and McClellan still had unbloodied reserves, Lee refused to retreat, and awaited the enemy's assaults on September 18. Again McClellan paused. Lee finally withdrew.

Most historians agree that Lee's army, after the fight at Manassas, was in no shape to conduct a successful invasion. Numerous tactical errors on Lee's part also added to his failed Maryland Campaign. Worst of all were the casualties: In one day Lee lost 27 percent of his army. McClellan's casualties amounted to 16 percent. As well, the Union victory gave Lincoln an opportunity he had been waiting for. Less than a week after the battle, Lincoln issued the Emancipation Proclamation, changing the nature of the war and how it was—and has been—perceived by the world.

One can see a pattern emerging: Lee's aggressive nature in battle was costing the Confederacy more than it could afford. It is confounding particularly for one reason. Lee's boyhood idol, and head of the family into which he had married, was George Washington, who had been faced with a very similar situation as commander of the Continental forces for which Lee's own father had fought. Usually out-numbered, facing a formidably equipped and supplied foe, and also fighting a war for independence, Washington realized that he didn't necessarily have to win the war—he just had to make sure he didn't lose it. This he did by tactical and strategic retreats and prolonging the war until the enemy's supply lines lengthened and were weakened by attacks, and their civilians tired of a seemingly never-ending war.

Why Lee did not adopt the strategy of his hero, who fought the prototype of the war Lee was to fight, is unknown—unless it was just in Lee's nature, unseen up to the moment of his taking field com-mand, to be aggressive and audacious.

Near the end of October, 1862, while in camp in Virginia, Lee received a letter from his wife with devastating news: Their twenty-three-year-old daughter Annie had died of typhoid in North Carolina. Annie seemed to be special to Lee since her disfiguring childhood accident. "Gentle Annie," he wrote of her. When his aide Walter Taylor delivered the mail, listened to his military orders, and left Lee's tent, he forgot something and returned a few moments later to find the always composed Lee "overcome with grief, an open letter in his hands."

In December of 1862, Lee at Fredericksburg, mostly on the defen-sive, took relatively few casualties, some 6 percent to his opponents' 11 percent.

About the same time, Rooney's newborn daughter died and became the second of Lee's grandchildren to be buried in Shockoe Cemetery that year.

Late winter and early spring of 1863 brought Lee more troubling news from his family: His wife's arthritis flared with the cold and damp of the season, and daughter Agnes suffered from pains in her face and neck, diagnosed as the catchall neuralgia. Daughter Mary Custis was trapped behind enemy lines. Though Lee worried about her, she turned down an escape when her friend from West Point days, Jeb Stuart, sent two scouts through the Yankee pickets to rescue her. Mary, until her last years, was the most independent of all Lee's daughters. No doubt Lee worried more about her than she did herself.

Lee, too, fell ill that March, suffering from what doctors diagnosed as a chest cold and sore throat, no doubt brought on from living, eating, and sleeping mostly in the outdoors since he had taken the field in June of 1862. He may have been misdiagnosed, since the pains in his chest would continue for the rest of his life. One historian makes the case that Lee probably suffered from pericarditis, as the pains radiated through his chest, back, and arms, as well as from hypertension, since his facial coloring grew more florid.

Come spring of 1863, Lee faced yet another Union commander, as Lincoln cast about for someone who could bring him a decisive victory in this war. Joseph Hooker developed an elaborate plan to outflank Lee west of Fredericksburg, near Chancellorsville. Again the audacious Lee split his army in the face of the enemy, sending Stonewall Jackson on an end-around to strike the Union forces on their exposed right flank. The attack took place late on May 2, 1863, and drove the Yankees from their positions, but at great cost, as Jackson was mortally wounded. The offensive did take a toll on the Confederates, however, who suffered 19 percent casualties to the defeated Union's 11 percent. Still, in Lee's mind, it gave him confidence to plan yet another invasion of the Northern states.

The fates chose June 9, 1863, for a confluence of events that would rattle Robert E. Lee's demeanor. First, the Yankees would surprise his most famous cavalry commander, Jeb Stuart, at Brandy Station, and nearly whip him. As it was, they severely wounded Lee's son Rooney, a general under Stuart's command. Lee personally saw that his youngest son, Robert, Jr., was detached from his service with the army to attend to his older brother. As if his cavalry arm nearly being beaten and his own son being wounded weren't enough, word came to him that daughter Agnes's suitor, handsome twenty-four-year-old Orton Williams, had been hanged as a spy in Franklin, Tennessee. Close friends of Agnes said she never recovered from the loss. Then, on June 26, Rooney, still recovering from his wound, was captured by the Yankees. His wife Charlotte, who had just lost two babies and seen her home burned to the ground, now broke down, certain her husband would die from the treatment he would receive as a prisoner of war. Lee would not learn of this last event until after the Gettysburg debacle.

During the month of June, 1863, Lee moved his army down (northward) along the Shenandoah Valley, using the Blue Ridge Mountains to the east as a screen.

By late June, advance elements were fanning out westward toward Bedford, Pennsylvania, northward to the Susquehanna River overlooking Harrisburg, the capital of Pennsylvania, and eastward, through York and to the Susquehanna at Columbia. When the Union Army was discovered near Gettysburg, about in the center of his spread-out divisions, they were ordered to concentrate there.

The first of three days of battle was a Confederate victory. Southern troops arrived more quickly to the fields of battle west, north, and east of the town, while northern units were still marching in from the south in an attempt to stay between the advancing Confederates and the Northern capital of Washington. Lee gave the directive to his subordinates not to bring on a general engagement, with his army spread out as it was, so we can only imagine what was running through Lee's mind as he rode toward Gettysburg from Cashtown to the sounds of a huge battle progressing. But upon arriving on the battlefield about 3:00 p.m. on July 1, 1863, as he rode over Seminary Ridge, he arrived just in time to see the Union Army collapsing in upon itself under Confederate pressure, streaming through the streets of the small town that lay before his feet. This vision of early victory may have set in his mind his subsequent tactics.

Lee's health, however, was a nagging problem. With Pennsylvania in the midst of cherry season, the soldiers gorged themselves on the ripe fruit. His own servant recalled that Lee, during the battle, made frequent trips to the latrine area. Far from being the modern joke that it is today, diarrhea during the Civil War was a killer, dehydrating the sufferer until he wasted away and died. Just the inconvenience to Lee, in his mid-fifties and trying to ride a horse for transportation, must have been maddeningly distracting. As well, the pains in his chest continued throughout the battle and campaign.

Though he issued orders on the afternoon of July 1 to Lt. Gen. Richard Ewell—to take the high ground south of the town (Culp's and Cemetery Hills), which would have deprived the Yankees of their tactical advantages—Ewell failed to launch the necessary assaults. Lee's orders included the phrase to attack "if practicable." One has to wonder, was Lee used to issuing orders to Stonewall Jackson? To Jackson these words would not have been taken as an excuse for inaction.

Lee spent the forenoon of July 2 inspecting the enemy's lines. He determined to attack both flanks simultaneously in order to prevent them from supporting one another. Almost immediately, Lt. Gen. James Longstreet opposed Lee's tactics. He had been under the impression, or so he wrote later, that the invasion would be strategically offensive (as all invasions are) but tactically defensive, finding a good position and forcing the Yankees to attack them. (At least one other Confederate general, Wade Hampton, claimed he also had hoped to fight on the defensive.) Longstreet wanted to flank the Union line to the south, establish entrenched positions between their army and Washington, and await an assault. Lee overruled him, stating aggressively: "If the enemy is there tomorrow, we must attack him."

That day, Longstreet was delayed in getting his troops in place for their role in assaulting the left of the Union line, and didn't launch his attacks until nearly 4:00 p.m., July 2. Ewell, who was to attack the other end of the Union line when he heard the sound of Longstreet's guns, for some reason never heard the cacophony to the south, and didn't launch his assault until Longstreet's was over. The Union line held against Longstreet's men at Little Round Top, and gave ground grudgingly through Devil's Den, the Peach Orchard, and the Wheatfield. Ewell's attack on Cemetery and Culp's Hills gained some success, until darkness brought a halt to the fighting. By dawn, Union troops, pulled from their trenches to support the fighting on the other end of the battlefield, returned to Culp's Hill. Fighting resumed, and while Lee's plan of occupying both ends of the Union line worked initially, Northerners eventually drove the Confederates off the hills, securing the Union right flank.

During the earlier fighting, however, elements of Longstreet's assault reached the Union center. Their officers reported back to Lee that it seemed weak. Lee concluded that in reinforcing his flanks, the Federal commander, General Meade, had weakened his center, and formulated a plan for a grand assault on the Union center.

The next day, July 3, would go down in military history as one of the greatest forlorn hopes of all time, its name becoming a euphemism for defeat and shattered dreams: Pickett's Charge. It would haunt Lee and generations of Southerners for the rest of their lives.

Prior to the assault of July 3, Longstreet argued with Lee yet again about the folly of sending 12,500 men across open fields to attack an enemy who had had two days to dig in. Years later, after Longstreet had become a Republican (in the wholly Democrat South), then made the mistake of criticizing Lee (akin to committing murder in the old Confederacy), he became one of the central targets for the "Lost Cause" movement, with the deceased Lee as its rallying point. Along with ruining the reputations of many fine former Confederate officers, it raised Lee to a level of godhood at which he would have been appalled.

After the slaughter that was Gettysburg, Lee began his retreat back into Virginia, never again to venture that far north. His casualty rates vary depending upon the historian, but even at their lowest estimate were astronomical: Some 30 to 37 percent of his army lay in the fields around Gettysburg, killed or wounded, or listed as missing—either captured, deserted, or liquefied by some type of ordnance. Union general Meade lost about 24 percent of his force. If nothing else, Gettysburg was a lesson in the folly of the frontal assault against massed troops behind field fortifications, armed with rifle muskets that could fire three times a minute with deadly accuracy to 350 yards.

The question becomes, after the second day's assaults failed, why would Lee not listen to the several Confederate officers who proposed maneuver as opposed to attack? Perhaps he saw a glimmer of hope to end the war in one grand assault; perhaps, as even he admitted, he believed too much in the ability of his own troops. Whatever his reasons for orchestrating the battle the way he did at Gettysburg, he was confronted by the fact that it was a tragic loss of manpower that the South could ill afford.

In addition to his depression from the defeat at Gettysburg, he received word that the Federals intended to hang a number of Confederate prisoners in retaliation if the Confederates executed some imprisoned Federals; one of the Confederates chosen by lot was Lee's son Rooney. After several nerve-racking days, cooler heads prevailed, realizing that a retaliatory orgy of hangings would result; however, to his father's continued concern, Rooney was still not on the list for prisoner exchange.

As well, he shared the shock with the rest of the South at the loss to the Confederacy of Vicksburg, Mississippi, on July 4, right after the defeat at Gettysburg. The "Father of Waters," the Mississippi River, which facilitated the flow of supplies across much of the Confederacy, was now in Federal control.

In August, Lee submitted his resignation as commander of the army after Gettysburg, taking full responsibility for the defeat. He cited a probable lack of confidence now by his officers and troops, though they were "too generous to exhibit it," and a general failure of his own health. He mentioned that he had not yet fully recovered from his "attack" from the spring (referring to his chest pains), and was less able to exert himself. It was rejected by President Jefferson Davis, because he could find no other with Lee's abilities.

Though the fall of 1863 brought news of the Confederate victory at Chickamauga, the loss of Chattanooga in November crushed Southern hopes.

And more worries brought on by the war loomed. The United States government began confiscating properties for nonpayment of taxes in occupied Southern territory, demanding that the taxes be paid in person as a particular hardship upon soldiers, whose homes were in the Federal armies' sphere of influence while they were away, fighting with the Confederate armies. Lee was in that situation with his own home, the Arlington house. He wrote to Custis that most of his money existed in Confederate States and North Carolina bonds, unacceptable as tax payments to the United States. Listing his other assets, he mentions his three horses, his watch, his clothing and camp equipage, and the estates of Custis's grandfather, all in the hands of the enemy or beyond Lee's reach. Any slaves Lee once owned were liberated, and the plantations in the family stripped of fences and houses. "The land alone remains a waste." In January of 1864, the government took Arlington from the Lee family, severing its last tie with George Washington.

December brought personal tragedy to Lee. Charlotte, Rooney's wife, whom Lee had embraced as if she were his own daughter, died the day before Christmas. To add to the heartache, though Rooney pleaded with the Yankees to let him see his wife before she died, with his brother Custis offering to take his place in prison, they refused. Charlotte was laid to rest next to the two small graves of Lee's grandchildren in Shockoe Cemetery.

Spring of 1864 brought Ulysses S. Grant to Virginia to confront Lee. In May Grant drove his army through the Wilderness, inflicting some 20 percent casualties upon Lee's army, while enduring 15 percent losses in his own. Lee could claim that he had stopped Grant in the Wilderness but for one thing: After the battle, Grant moved south.

After just a day's march, the armies were at it again, fighting for a strategic crossroads en route to Richmond at Spotsylvania Court House, where the bloodletting continued on an unprecedented scale. Though both armies lost excessively, Lee's was the army that could least afford it.

More bad news, touching both personal and professional emotions, was brought to Lee. Jeb Stuart, whom he had known since his West Point days when Stuart would visit his daughter Mary, whom Lee took to Harpers Ferry to quell the insurrectionist John Brown, and who, as Lee put it, "never brought me a piece of false information," was dead after being wounded defending Richmond.

Toward the end of May, during the fighting at the North Anna River, Lee became so debilitated with an intestinal illness that he took to riding in a carriage instead of on Traveller, and was tent-bound for a period. It did not pass quickly, but lingered for several days, limiting his movements on the battlefields to where he could go in a carriage.

Yet Grant continued southward.

At Cold Harbor, near one of the battlefields fought over by Lee in 1862, Grant ordered the one assault he said he regretted more than any other. Sadly, his veterans knew what was coming: Before leaving their positions to attack Lee's well-entrenched Confederates, they were seen sewing small tags inside their blue jackets with their names and hometowns handwritten on the tags; they wanted their bodies to be identified and their families to be told where they had died and were buried. Some seven thousand became casualties in less than a half-hour.

Grant, after building one of the longest pontoon bridges in military history, crossed the James River, moving southward to threaten Richmond and Petersburg. By mid-June, 1864, Lee's army was under siege at Petersburg. Even Lee knew that now it was just a matter of time.

For the next nine months, Grant continued to stretch his lines farther to the west. He knew that Lee's—and the South's—manpower was limited. During that time other Confederate armies in the western theater endured defeats, the most grievous coming at Franklin, Tennessee, at the end of November, when John Bell Hood, formerly under Lee, recklessly sent men to their deaths in an assault that made Pickett's Charge at Gettysburg seem small by comparison. Hood sent some twenty thousand men down a gentle slope of two miles to attack entrenched Federals south of the town, killing six of his general officers and wounding seven more, and losing over six thousand of the attacking force, a total of 23 percent loss to his army.

Lee's daughter Agnes chose the end of March, 1865, to visit friends in Petersburg, despite Lee's warnings to her. Around that time, fighting flared on the westernmost flank of Lee's army, and a vital road junction called Five Forks fell to Union infantry and cavalry commanded by Philip Sheridan. The entire Confederate siege line, from Five Forks to Richmond, had to be abandoned, as did the capital of the Confederacy. Lee led his army on a week of running fights as the Federal army attempted to cut him off from supplies and a unification with Johnston's army in North Carolina. Agnes escaped Petersburg only to arrive home in Richmond in time to see the city burned and occupied by the Yankees.

On April 9, 1865, Lee's army—or what was left of it—was trapped at Appomattox Court House, and Lee surrendered the Army of Northern Virginia. Perhaps the finest thing he did was to shut down talk from subordinate officers that they should take to the mountains and conduct a guerrilla-style war within their own states, a catastrophic move that would have ensured sectional warfare for generations.

Returning to his family in Richmond, he still worried about his youngest son Rob, who finally showed up, the last to return from the war. Rob and Rooney began farming what was left of their inheritances, and Lee turned down several job offers from companies that only wanted him for his name.

Agnes came down with typhoid fever and Lee feared that he might lose yet another daughter to illness. Her younger sister Mildred nursed her back to health. Lee and his family remained in a small cottage loaned to them by a sympathetic benefactor.

In August of 1865, Lee got a job offer he felt he could accept: the presidency of Washington College in Lexington. Considering the position, he saw it as a way to influence, through education, future generations of Southerners. His hiring proved a boon to enrollment, as survivors of the war sought to continue their education in Lee's presence, or teach at the same college Lee now headed. Custis got a teaching position at the Virginia Military Academy, but the rest of the family didn't arrive in Lexington until late fall. The furnishings were sparse, but Rob, who had accompanied his mother and sisters, wrote that they were all grateful and happy to be home—the only one they'd had for four years.

At last Lee could enjoy a modicum of mental rest. He was settled in an occupation that was satisfying to his soul, and he knew where the members of his beloved family were. He finally had a home life, and could provide a relatively good income to sustain it. But by 1867, when he was only sixty years old, his health began to fail.

In part, it was the heart condition that had begun in the spring of 1863, once diagnosed as a chest cold, but which may have been an inflammation of the heart sac—pericarditis. Even he acknowledged the stresses he had been under, first during the war as the Confederacy's most famous leader, then under Reconstruction, in attempting to maintain his self-control as an example to other Southerners. He often referenced the strain, especially in the last months of the war. But whenever someone would bring up the name of Jeb Stuart, he would brighten. He mentioned long rides on Traveller as being therapeutic, helping him to take his mind off of things.

The next years brought more fatigue for Lee, even when doing the simplest things, yet he was still called upon to testify in the trial of Jefferson Davis in Richmond, shortly after attending son Rooney's second marriage ceremony in Petersburg. Visits to both places brought back memories of the long siege.

In March of 1869, he and his wife learned that the United States government would keep the Washington relics confiscated from Arlington. He expressed hope that more people would learn from them of Washington's virtues.

In May he visited his one-time adversary Ulysses S. Grant in the White House, on a social visit. He also visited what he considered his hometown of Alexandria. He attended a church council meeting, taking him to another old battlefield town with hard memories of wartime destruction: Fredericksburg. Consulting with his doctors, he made a trip to one of the several therapeutic "springs" in Virginia, where he learned of the sudden death of his brother, Smith Lee. Though he missed the funeral in Alexandria, it gave him an excuse to see Ravensworth again, one of the family plantations left to his sons, and visit the very room where he'd stood forty years before, when his beloved mother died. "It seems now but yesterday," he said to Rob.

A visit to Rooney via Richmond was decided upon. Afterward Lee came down with a vicious cold that hung on through the fall, until December. Now, Lee had trouble breathing with just the least bit of exertion. Walking the short distance from the president's home (a new one built by the school just for him and Mary) to his office in the chapel took his breath and gave him near constant pain. Yet, he felt one more duty call.

He traveled south again with Agnes, first, to see the grave of his daughter Annie, then to see the grave of the man whose reputation Lee was painfully and acutely aware of, for much of his life: his father. They stayed in Savannah for almost a month, sailing to Cumberland Island where his father was buried. He wrote to Mary that the trip was pleasant and that he was feeling stronger, although he had chest pains whenever he walked, and occasionally experienced pain even when at rest, a new symptom.

In the spring he sat for sculptor Edward Valentine and posed for some photographs. He visited a doctor in Baltimore, who suggested treatment for "rheumatic excitement," but nothing for Lee's heart. On his way home he stopped in Alexandria to consult his lawyer about getting some of the Arlington property returned to fulfill his father-in-law's will, bequeathing money to Lee's daughters, still bound to his duty and worrying about his girls.

When the school year began in mid-September, 1870, he assumed his duties. On September 28 he wrote to a friend that he was feeling better after a trip to the hot springs. The pains in his chest seemed to be less, and he was hopeful of even more improvement. The weather in Lexington had turned cold and rainy, and at 4:00 p.m. he attended a meeting at the unheated Episcopal Church just down the hill from his home. The meeting went long, the vestrymen discussing the $55 they were short to complete Dr. Pendleton's salary. Pendleton was one of Lee's former officers. Finally a voice said softly, "I will give that sum." It was Lee. The meeting was adjourned.

Lee walked through a hard rain to his house, where Mary and his daughters were impatiently waiting for him. His wife scolded him for being uncharacteristically late. Lee hung up his cloak and took his place at the head of the table to say grace, as always, but no words came. He sat. The look on his face told Mary that he had already resigned himself to this one last call to duty.

He lingered for two weeks. Slowly sinking, at the end he was back on the battlefield, ordering A. P. Hill, who had been with Lee in nearly all his battles, and had been killed outside of Petersburg, to come up with his troops. On October 12, 1870, Lee died. His last words were, "Strike the tent."

Lee's participation as commander of the largest army of the Confederacy lasted just shy of two years and ten months, a short span for his six decades of life. But it is the event with which he is most associated. Because of it he became a tragic figure to the South, a symbol of the "Lost Cause" of the Confederacy. Even in death, his country refused to let him go.

24

JOHN WILKES BOOTH: CURSED IN VIRGINIA

The twelve-foot skiff rode up on the muddy shore. A man got out and pulled it farther on land, then turned to help another steady himself on his crutches and work his way out of the shifting boat onto the sandy shore. Finally, John Wilkes Booth stepped foot in Virginia. Now, he thought, he would be hailed as a hero of the South.

He believed he finally would be safe in Virginia after his heinous crime, hitherto unknown in America: the assassination of the president. Wasn't Virginia one of the more important states in the Confederacy? Wouldn't the citizens proclaim him a hero? Wouldn't the network of Confederate agents he knew rally around him and assist him in his escape to Mexico? Didn't he invoke their state motto as he struck the fatal blow?

Just as he was mistaken in his estimation of how the nation would receive his action—what he thought of as ridding the country of a tyrant—he was also completely wrong about how those in Virginia would react to his deed. He would not be heralded as a hero but as a liability as he tried to cross through war-weary Virginia on his way to Mexico. But at this point in his escape, despite the intense pain of a broken left leg, he must have felt relieved just to arrive in the Old Dominion.

He had been on the run for over a week. At about 10:15 p.m. on Good Friday, April 14, he had leapt onto the stage of Ford's Theatre in Washington from the president's box, shouted *Sic semper tyrannis!* to the audience, as if he were part of the play. He had run to a waiting horse located in the alley behind the theater, and galloped off into the spring night. This, of course, after shooting President Abraham Lincoln in the back of the head.

His escape had taken him across the Potomac River into Maryland. There he met up with David Herold and continued his ride south, leaving behind him a dying president and utter pandemonium in the nation's capital. Another conspirator had attempted to assassinate Lincoln's secretary of state, William H. Seward. When word got out, fear spread that it was a wide conspiracy to behead the federal government. Gen. Ulysses S. Grant had left Washington for New Jersey, but it was feared that his life was also in danger, as were the lives of Secretary of War Stanton, Vice President Johnson, and God only knew how many others. Officials were concerned that there might be the artificial spread of disease via germs in major cities of the North, that the water supply of New York City was to be poisoned, and that Northern cities were the targets of arsonists. Since the military defeat of the Confederacy, it was obvious to many who was behind these sinister plots: disgruntled Southerners.

Booth and Herold had made their way, mostly at night, through Surrattsville, Maryland, to the house of a physician to have Booth's broken leg set, then toward Bryantown. A cold front moved in that Easter Sunday morning, with a hard, freezing breeze. Eventually the two arrived at a godforsaken wilderness called Zekiah Swamp. With the help of a guide they passed through the swamp and made it to a Confederate agent, who took them to a pine thicket to hide. Newspapers were brought to Booth. The articles slammed him and his act, among other things, as the worst thing that could have happened to the South. For several days Booth and Herold remained hidden in the thicket, the actor fuming over the reception of what he thought was a patriotic act against a despot.

Finally, another Confederate operative, under the cover of darkness on April 20, led them to the Potomac. Supplying them with a skiff and compass bearings, he helped them get out into the river. Union gunboats, the tide, fog, darkness, and a bend in the river were all against them. As well, Booth apparently was a better actor than a navigator, since he was in charge of the compass and candle with which to read it. Instead of rowing directly across the river to Virginia, they ended up back on the Maryland shore at Nanjemoy Creek. Two nights later they tried the crossing again.

The result of the second attempt to reach Virginia was successful. They reached Mathias Point on the Virginia shore of the river. They had been told to get in touch with a Mrs. Quesenberry on Machodoc Creek. Once again, their navigational skills were wanting. Instead they struck Gambo Creek, and were forced into that tributary by a patrolling Union gunboat. Herold set out on foot to find the Quesenberry house.

Elizabeth Quesenberry, for being a Confederate sympathizer, was not very sympathetic to the scruffy stranger. She refused to supply him with a horse, and wanted him off her property. As Herold was leaving, she did offer to send him some food.

Apparently, Quesenberry was concerned about her own future. With the war over and the Confederate military disbanded, Yankee patrols would have no resistance. She was afraid of how she would be perceived by Federals looking for an assassin. According to historians, she was well-connected to the Confederate spy network along the river. No doubt by now she had heard of Lincoln's assassination. In fact, she sent the food to Booth and Herold via two others sympathetic to the Confederate cause. After they ate, the men moved the two fugitives along the pipeline, and they eventually ended up at a house named Cleydael, owned by one of the wealthiest men in Virginia, Dr. Richard H. Stuart.

Stuart was rich and well-connected. Cleydael was his second, "country" home, where the daughters of his cousin Robert E. Lee once stayed when they were forced out of their home in Arlington. Though Stuart came highly recommended by Confederate sympathizers, he, like Mrs. Quesenberry, wanted nothing to do with the strangers who rode up after supper on April 23. Perhaps because of his connection with the Lees, he had been watched throughout the war by Yankee spies. He even spent a few months on a prison ship, an experience he was reluctant to repeat.

So when the strangers arrived, he was willing to give them food, but wanted to hear nothing about them. He went outside to talk to the men who had delivered them, but learned little from them about their identities, just that they had been told to seek him out. He told the men that they must take the strangers elsewhere.

Inside, however, a former Confederate staff officer recognized them, and they evidently discussed the assassination with Booth, who admitted that the killing of the president was all conceived and planned in one day.

When Stuart returned to his house, he all but forced the strangers out of his home and on to the small cabin of an African-American family. Booth and Herold pushed their way inside and threatened William Lucas with violence. Lucas and his family stayed outside for the night. On the morning of April 24, the conspirators paid Lucas for a ride in his wagon, driven by his son, to Port Conway on the Rappahannock River.

Near noon they arrived at the ferry crossing of the river at Port Conway. By now Herold was introducing Booth as his brother, John W. Boyd (to coincide with Booth's tattooed "JWB" visible on his hand) and himself as David E. Boyd. As they waited for the ferry which was across the river at Port Royal, three former Confederate soldiers rode up. In the ensuing conversation, the three revealed that they were associated with John S. Mosby's celebrated partisan rangers. Herold lied and said they were formerly of A. P. Hill's corps, and that his "brother" had been wounded at Petersburg. Perhaps Herold just couldn't keep up a lie very long, or perhaps he wanted what he thought was fame, but he eventually admitted to one of the three former Confederates that it was they who had assassinated the Northern president.

Once across the river, the five men stopped at the home of Miss Sarah Jane Peyton. Asked if she would take care of a wounded ex-Confederate soldier, she agreed, but when Booth made his appearance, she changed her mind. After his time on the run, camping in the woods and suffering from a broken leg, he no longer had the matinee idol looks he'd once enjoyed. Miss Peyton was suspicious, and gave the excuse that she was alone and that it wouldn't be proper for two gentlemen to move in under the same roof. Booth, Herold, and the three former soldiers rode on, heading south.

After the poor reception Booth had received everywhere he went in Virginia, it appears he was growing despondent; he told one of his companions that he would not be taken alive—that he would commit suicide before that would happen.

Several miles south of Port Royal the party rode up to the farmhouse of Richard Garrett. The Garrett family members in the home at the time included his wife, her sister, and nine children, including two older sons who were returning Confederate veterans. One of the riders, Willie Jett, asked Garrett if he would care for a wounded Confederate soldier. Garrett agreed, and into his house limped the most wanted man in America. Jett, Herold, and the other two soldiers rode on toward Bowling Green, Virginia, leaving John Wilkes Booth alone at the Garrett farm.

In the meantime, Union cavalry had crossed the Rappahannock to Port Royal. While at the Rappahannock River crossing, they had confirmed that Booth had traveled that way, and also learned that one Willie Jett was with them, and probably heading to meet up with his sweetheart in Bowling Green. The cavalry rode south, passing the Garrett farm on their way. At nearly midnight, they found Jett sleeping at a hotel in the town and dragged him out of bed. Jett said he knew where the man they were looking for was, and offered to lead them to him.

Earlier, before the cavalry had passed, Herold had returned to the farm and told Booth he was ready to go home, exhausted from living on the run. Booth calmed him down, and the two asked to spend another night at the farm. By now the Garrett boys had grown suspicious and told them they had to sleep in the tobacco barn. It had a lock on the door, and they could watch the two without fearing for their family.

It was the middle of the night when Jett led the Yankee cavalry to the Garrett farm. Garrett answered the door. He apparently wasn't answering questions quickly enough, so the cavalrymen procured a rope and threatened to string him up. One of Garrett's sons led them to the barn and they forced him to enter and parley with Booth and Herold. A threat was made to Booth from outside that if he didn't surrender, the cavalry would burn him out of the barn in fifteen minutes. Booth, as was typical, wanted to talk some more; Herold wanted to surrender. They argued, and officials from outside repeated their threats to fire the building. Booth called out that he was crippled, and all he wanted was a fair fight. His time had dwindled to five minutes. Still, he told the official to draw his men up in a line so that Booth could fight his way out. Perhaps in his mind Booth saw a chance for one great last theatrical scene. Perhaps he was looking for what modern criminalists call "suicide by cop." Regardless, the soldiers set fire to the barn.

That did it for Herold; he didn't want to be roasted alive. He rushed to the door, was captured, and tied to a locust tree outside the house.

Booth hobbled about inside the barn, flames adding a lurid backdrop to his dramatic final act. To further upset the tragedy Booth was trying to create, a strange character entered and ruined his grand finale. Boston Corbett, a sergeant with the cavalry surrounding the barn, was a former hatter from New York. After losing his wife and child to death, he rose out of his depression by becoming a devout Christian. So devout, in fact, that after he was tempted by some prostitutes, he castrated himself. No more of that kind of temptation for him.

Years later, he found himself peering through a crack in the Garretts' tobacco barn at the most wanted man in the country. Corbett saw Booth lifting the carbine he was carrying, so he put his own pistol through the crack and fired. Booth went down, Corbett's .44 caliber bullet having passed into the right side of his neck and through his spinal column. Men from outside rushed into the barn and carried the limp actor out to place him on the grass. As the fire consumed the barn, they moved Booth to the porch of the Garrett farmhouse.

Though Booth seemed to be aware of his surroundings, he was virtually paralyzed from the neck wound down, and having trouble breathing, swallowing, and speaking. He whispered that he wanted water, but choked when he couldn't swallow. He indicated that he needed to be alternately turned on his sides, which his captors did. He begged in a low voice, "Kill me," which went unheeded. For nearly two hours, the assassin of Abraham Lincoln suffered, slowly suffocating on the Garrett porch until sunrise.

In a low whisper, still the dramatist, he asked that his captors tell his mother that he did it for his country; that he had died for his country. Finally, he asked that they lift his hands so that he might see them. They did so and he whispered, "Useless . . . useless." He died soon after.

They took Booth's body from the Garrett farm to Belle Plains, east of Fredericksburg on Potomac Creek, where he left the state of Virginia for Washington. On the ironclad *Montauk*, on April 27, Booth's remains were identified, photographed, and examined by army surgeons. He would spend several years buried under the floor of the Old Arsenal Prison (now Fort Lesley J. McNair in Washington), while his brother wrote to Ulysses S. Grant and Lincoln's successor, President Johnson, asking that the remains be returned to the family. Eventually they were, and John Wilkes Booth now lies in an unmarked grave in the Booth family plot, Green Mount Cemetery in Baltimore.

BIBLIOGRAPHY

BOOKS AND ARTICLES

Bonekemper, Edward H., III. *How Robert E. Lee Lost the Civil War.* Fredericksburg, VA: Sergeant Kirkland's Press, 1997.

Coulling, Mary P. *The Lee Girls.* Winston-Salem, NC: John F. Blair, Publisher, 1987.

Donnelly, Mark P., and Daniel Diehl. *Pirates of Virginia.* Mechanicsburg, PA: Stackpole Books, 2012.

Dowdey, Clifford. *Lee.* New York: Bonanza Books, 1965.

Farwell, Byron. *Ball's Bluff: A Small Battle and Its Long Shadow.* McLean, VA: EPM Publications, 1990.

Felder, Paula S. *Fielding Lewis and the Washington Family: A Chronicle of 18th Century Fredericksburg.* (No publisher listed.)

Gallagher, Gary W. *The Battle of Chancellorsville* (National Park Civil War Series). Fort Washington, PA: Eastern National, 1995.

——, ed. *The Spotsylvania Campaign: Military Campaign of the Civil War.* Chapel Hill and London: University of North Carolina Press, 1998.

Gray, Thomas R. *The Confessions of Nat Turner.* Baltimore: Thomas R. Gray, 1831.

Guiley, Rosemary Ellen. *The Encyclopedia of Demons and Demonology.* New York: Checkmark Books, 2009.

———. *Harper's Encyclopedia of Mystical and Paranormal Experience*. New York: HarperCollins, 1991.

Harrison, Noel G. *Fredericksburg Civil War Sites, December 1862–April 1865*. Vol. II. Lynchburg, VA: H. E. Howard, Inc., 1995.

Higginson, Thomas Wentworth. "Nat Turner's Insurrection," *The Atlantic* (August 1861), Library of Congress.

Howard, William F. *The Battle of Ball's Bluff: "The Leesburg Affair," October 21, 1861*. Lynchburg, VA: H. E. Howard, Inc., 1994.

Kelso, William M. *Jamestown: The Buried Truth*. Charlottesville and London: University of Virginia Press, 2006.

Lee, Marguerite DuPont. *Virginia Ghosts*. Berryville VA: Virginia Book Company (reprint), 1966.

Mapp, Alf J. *Frock Coats and Epaulets: Psychological Portraits of Confederate Military Leaders*. Lanham, MD: Hamilton Press, 1987.

Mertz, Gregory A. "Upton's Attack and the Defense of Dole's Salient Spotsylvania Court House, VA, May 10, 1864," *Blue & Gray* Magazine, Vol. XVIII, Issue 6 (Summer 2001).

Morris, Roy Jr., *Sheridan: The Life and Wars of General Phil Sheridan*. New York: Vintage Books, 1992.

Oates, Stephen. *The Fires of Jubilee: Nat Turner's Fierce Rebellion*. New York: New American Library, 1975.

O'Reilly, Francis Augustin. *The Fredericksburg Campaign: Winter War on the Rappahannock*. Baton Rouge: Louisiana State University Press, 2003.

Pfanz, Donald C. "American Golgotha: The Creation and Early History of Fredericksburg National Cemetery," *The Journal of Fredericksburg History,* Vol. 9. Fredericksburg, VA: Historic Fredericksburg Foundation, 2005.

Rhea, Gordon C. *The Battles for Spotsylvania Court House and the Road to Yellow Tavern May 7–12, 1864.* Baton Rouge: Louisiana State University Press, 1997.

Taylor, L. B., Jr. "The Headless Blue Lady of Charlotte Street," *The Ghosts of Fredericksburg and Nearby Environs.* Williamsburg, VA: L. B. Taylor, Jr., 1991.

——. *The Ghosts of Virginia,* Vol. I. Williamsburg, VA: L. B. Taylor Jr., 1993.

WEBSITES

"America's Wars: US Casualties and Veterans," InfoPlease (www. infoplease.com/ipa/A0004615.html), accessed July 26, 2016.

"Appomattox," CivilWar@Smithsonian (www.civilwar.si.edu/ appomattox_furniture.html), accessed September 22, 2016.

"Chesapeake and Ohio Canal," Wikipedia (https://en.wikipedia.org/ wiki/Chesapeake_and_Ohio_Canal), accessed July 26, 2016.

"Colonial Williamsburg," Revolutionary Day (www.revolutionaryday .com/usroute60/williamsburg/default.htm), accessed August 27, 2016.

"Court Ruling on Anthony Johnson and His Servant," Encyclopedia Virginia (www.encyclopediavirginia.org/Court_Ruling_on_ Anthony_Johnson_and_His_Servant_1655), accessed August 24, 2016. "The Dahlgren Papers Revisited," HistoryNet (www.historynet .com/the-dahlgren-papers-revisited.htm/1), accessed August 6, 2016.

"Early Jamestown Settlement," Encyclopedia Virginia (www.encyc lopediavirginia.org/Jamestown_Settlement_Early), accessed July 28, 2016.

"Jamestown: 1609–10: 'Starving Time,' " (nationalhumanitiescenter
.org/pds/amerbegin/settlement/text2/JamestownPercyRelation.pdf),
accessed July 28, 2016.

"John Casor," Wikipedia (https://en.wikipedia.org/wiki/John_Casor),
accessed August 24, 2016.

"The McLean House: Site of the Surrender," Appomattox Court House,
National Park Service (www.nps.gov/apco/mclean-house.htm),
accessed September 21, 2016.

Martin, Samuel J. "Captain Judson Kilpatrick," www.historynet.com/
union-captain-judson-kilpatrick.htm, accessed August 8, 2016.
(Originally published in the February 2000 issue of *Civil War Times*
magazine.)

"Mexican-American War: Aftermath & Legacy," About Education
(militaryhistory.about.com/od/mexicanamericanwar/a/MexicanEnd
.htm), accessed July 26, 2016.

"Murder and Mayhem Ride the Rails," HistoryNet (www.history
net.com/murder-and-mayhem-ride-the-rails-union-soldiers
-rampage-in-virginia.htm/1), accessed August 26, 2016. "Nat
Turner's Insurrection," *The Atlantic* (www.theatlantic.com/magazine/
archive/1861/08/nat-turners-insurrection/308736/), accessed August
19, 2016.

"The Murderer," Boothie Barn (https://boothiebarn.com/), accessed
between September 22, 2016 and October 15, 2016.

INDEX

ABOUT THE AUTHOR

Mark Nesbitt was a National Park Service Ranger/Historian for five years at Gettysburg before starting his own research and writing company. Since then he has published fourteen books including the national award–winning Ghosts of Gettysburg series. His stories have been seen on History Channel, A&E, Discovery Channel, Travel Channel, *Unsolved Mysteries,* and numerous regional television shows, and heard on *Coast to Coast AM* and regional radio. In 1994, he created the commercially successful Ghosts of Gettysburg Candlelight Walking Tours® and in 2006, the Ghosts of Fredericksburg Tours.